DESIGN FOR WHOLENESS

Brother Loughlan Sofield, ST, is Senior Editor of *Human Development* magazine and conducts workshops around the world on topics of ministry and psychology. He is co-author of *Collaborative Ministry* (Ave Maria Press), *Inside Christian Community* and *Developing the Parish as a Community of Service* (both from Human Development). Sofield is Councilor General of the Missionary Servants of the Most Holy Trinity.

Sister Carroll Juliano, SHCJ, is Director of Life Planning for Ministry in Summit, NJ, and has conducted workshops in North America, Europe and Africa on life planning, ministry and personal development. She is the co-author of *Collaborative Ministry* (Ave Maria Press) and has contributed articles to *Human Development, Today's Parish,* and *Review for Religious.*

Sister Rosine Hammett, CSC, Ph.D., is Co-Director of the Consultation Center for the Congregation of Holy Cross. As a therapist, lecturer, communications consultant and facilitator of personal growth groups, she has worked with men and women religious and laity in North and South America, Asia and in Israel. She is co-author of *Inside Christian Community* (Human Development) and has published articles in *Human Development* and *Sisters Today.*

SOFIELD·JULIANO·HAMMETT

DESIGN FOR WHOLENESS

Dealing With Anger
Learning to Forgive
Building Self-Esteem

AVE MARIA PRESS
Notre Dame, Indiana 46556

© 1990 by Ave Maria Press, Notre Dame, IN 46556

International Standard Book Number: 0-87793-430-4

Library of Congress Catalog Card Number: 90-82098

Cover and text design by Elizabeth J. French

Cover photograph by Vernon Sigl

Printed and bound in the United States of America.

To
Mal and Ray
Georgeanna and Eleanor
Henry, Bill and Olivia
who are life-giving for us

Contents

Acknowledgments

We are deeply grateful and appreciative to the numerous friends whose efforts in a variety of ways have contributed to this book:

To the Jesuit Educational Center for Human Development, especially James Gill, S.J., Linda Amadeo, and John Murray, S.J., for their significant contribution to the development of the material.

To the staffs of the Ministries Center for the Laity, Brooklyn, New York, and the Trinity Ministries Center, Stirling, New Jersey, for their contribution to some of the material.

To Marlene Debole without whose invaluable secretarial assistance this book would not have been possible; and Mary Pat Schlickenmaier, Marian Joseph Cain, C.S.C., and Mary Davis for the office support services they rendered.

To the following people who willingly gave of their time and talents to critique the manuscript in its various stages: Jane Bigelow, S.H.C.J., Donald Doyle, Eleanor Doyle, Jonathan Doyle, Maria Beata Heaney, C.S.C., Peter Holden, S.T., Georgeanna Juliano, Helena Mayer, S.H.C.J., Ambrose McCraken, C.S.C., Hilary Mettes, S.T., Domingo Rodriguez, S.T., Claire Smith, S.H.C.J., Malachy Sofield, S.T., Mary Sofield and Raymond Sofield.

Introduction

"I have come so that you may have life and have it to the full" (Jn 10:10). This message of Christ is clear and direct. The reason Christ came, and his desire for all people, is that we be filled with life. The call to fullness of life in Christ involves a mystery of being, the mystery of love. Each of us is called by name to the fullness of that life in Christ through community and in ministry. In the Old Testament, vocation or call refers to God's calling us into existence. Through this call we are invited to cooperate with God in the ongoing process of creation, to enter into a covenant relationship with God to be life-giving. The hunger for life and for life-giving relationships and situations is at the core of human existence.

In the past several years we have been conducting workshops on the topics of collaborative ministry and community. Our work has taken us to many different countries and many different cultures. We consistently discover women and men responding to the call to fullness of life and striving to live out the values of family, ministry and community, but encountering difficulties and at times almost losing hope. People often express ministry, family or community as more life-draining than life-giving. We have discovered two key issues that affect the life-giving quality of relationships: anger and low self-esteem.

This book is an attempt to offer insights and observations for dealing with these two key issues and related areas. The purpose of the book is to explore the life-giving potential of these issues by encouraging further growth through reflection questions, practical examples and exercises. While the book is directed toward anyone trying to live the Christian life to the fullest, it will be especially helpful to those in ministry.

The inability or unwillingness to deal with anger results in ineffective ministry or, worse, broken, hurting, lifeless people. Of course, anger is a difficult emotion for most people in most societies. It is our conviction that anger is especially difficult for those in ministry. Chapter 1 presents a model for understanding anger. When people understand and demythologize anger, they can reduce its potential destructiveness. Only then can anger become life-giving. Chapter 2 presents a case study that explains some basic principles about anger and helps the reader to examine personal beliefs about anger.

The most effective way of dealing with anger is to learn to forgive. Forgiveness is much more complex and difficult than often imagined. Chapter 3 deals with the process and resistance to forgiveness. It is when anger and forgiveness are paired that anger can foster and generate life. Both are essential to building relationships, while both arouse fear of annihilation.

In analyzing the similarities in the issues of anger and forgiveness, we find a single thread running through that unites them and explains the often paralyzing fear that is present. The issue common to both is self-esteem. A positive, healthy self-esteem is fundamental to effective, life-giving community and ministry. In fact, our basic premise is that to be a life-giving, generative person, an individual must have developed a capacity for relationships with self and with others that can support and sustain a good sense of personal worth and value. When individuals striving for community and collaborative ministry possess a high degree of self-esteem, there is a greater opportunity for the life-giving quality to be realized. Chapter 4 proposes a model for understanding and increasing self-esteem.

The final chapter looks at the point where anger and self-esteem meet: dialogue in our relationships. We deal with anger through mature dialogue with others. Self-esteem is developed in the context of relationships through dialogue. This chapter looks at some dynamics, presents a developmental model for dialogue and offers some exercises for dialogue.

Where we have used stories or examples to illustrate our text, we have been careful to maintain confidentiality and anonymity through changing any identifying circumstances. Also, though in all of this the authors have in general had similar experiences, there may be a few examples that belong to one author only but which are supported by like experiences by all of us.

It is our hope that this book will encourage and challenge the reader to further steps in the lifelong journey toward fullness of life in Christ.

Carroll Juliano, S.H.C.J.
Rosine Hammett, C.S.C.
Loughlan Sofield, S.T.

Chapter One

Anger: A Threat to Life

The emotion of anger is a single thread that weaves its way through all areas of life. When it becomes tangled or knotted, the repercussions have a ripple effect. How people communicate and relate in family, work, ministry or community is affected by how they handle the emotion of anger—their own or others'.

Most people have read articles on anger, listened to lectures on coping with it and perhaps even talked with friends about the impact anger has on their lives. Yet anger remains an Achilles' heel for many. Several years ago in the *New York Times*, columnist Jane E. Brody wrote that "anger is without question the most apparent, most talked about and most poorly handled emotion in modern American society."[1] Our experience in working with people throughout the world supports and underlines the fact that anger continues to be an area of stress in all situations of life.

While it may be an area of stress, anger does not have to be a debilitating force. Stress is a two-edged sword. There is stress in life that drains energy and produces tension. There is another type of stress (*eustress*)[2] that is a positive and creative life-force. Cultural conditioning, family upbringing or religious education have led many Christians to categorize anger as negative stress. The beliefs that each person holds about anger as an emotion play an important role in determining how one will subsequently deal with anger. For Christians called to fullness of life in Christ the challenge is to see anger as a positive force and a source of personal and interpersonal growth, not as something to be feared and avoided.

In this chapter we examine the emotion of anger from its

source to its expression, and then make recommendations. Chapter 2 features a case study as a basis for exploring some general principles about anger. The approach is to develop three paradigms. Paradigm One tracks anger to its source and ultimately to its expression. This is based on our belief that a person can deal effectively with anger only when there is awareness of the normal dynamics involved in the emotion.

Paradigm Two challenges individuals to take more responsibility for anger, emphasizing the fact that the causes of anger are not external to oneself—the external factors are only the stimuli or catalysts. Ultimately, each person must learn to accept the fact that it is not the situation that produces any emotion, including anger. Rather, it is the personal beliefs that one projects onto a situation that ultimately determine the resulting emotion.

The concern of most people is how to deal effectively and constructively with the inevitable anger in their lives. Paradigm Three guides people through a process of acceptance of the emotion, followed by reflection and dialogue leading to constructive action.

We pose three questions for the reader to use as a backdrop in the following discussion of anger:

Why is anger such a difficult emotion for so many of us?

What can I do to assist myself and others to deal with anger so that it strengthens rather than destroys relationships?

When I experience anger, how can it become life-giving for me and others?

Dynamics of Anger

A television program offered some important lessons about anger. The show centered around several women and men in their middle twenties who worked together. They were reminiscing, telling stories of times when as adolescents or teenagers each one had been a victim of a peer who had bullied him or her. The last young man to speak related his story, which ended with a bully destroying his uncle's prized car. The uncle had generously allowed the use of the car for his nephew's senior prom. The young man loved his uncle and would never intentionally do anything to hurt him. Turning over this prized possession into his hands was a sign of his uncle's trust in him. When the teenager arrived at the prom, the bully shoved the youth away from the car, got into the driver's seat and rammed the car into a wall. The youth was furious at the bully and ashamed of himself for doing nothing to prevent the damage. He felt that he had betrayed his uncle's trust.

In relating the incident years later, it was obvious to his friends that he was still angry at the bully and with himself for doing nothing to prevent the accident. The conversation with his colleagues stirred up all the old feelings of anger, and the young man decided to go home and settle the score. He visited his uncle with the intention of finding this bully and finally getting revenge. The wise uncle offered the young man some sound advice: "Look, forget about the whole thing. It happened eight years ago. It's over and done. You have a choice: You can let your anger eat away at you, or you can let go of it and continue on with the rest of your life."

This is the choice that each person faces every time anger is experienced. The emotion will perdure and continue to destroy as long as we choose to nurture it.

What caused this young man to feel angry? Why is he still angry now, when the event occurred years before? The story touches upon an almost universal experience. For which of us cannot look back upon an incident in our own lives when we felt angry and wanted revenge, yet never really resolved those angry feelings? Even now in the present if we recall that incident, those angry feelings again come to the surface. Think about such a situation in your own life. Keep this situation in mind as we move through the path of anger.

It is useful to note the flow of anger as it moves from origin to expression. We believe that people can better handle anger when there is an understanding of what happens when the emotion of anger is experienced. In training counselors we observe how people want ready-made answers: "What do I do if . . . ?" It is difficult to convince students that if they know what is happening, then they can logically decide what to do. There are no ready-made, pat answers for handling anger. The key to dealing with anger effectively is to understand its origins. Through the analysis and understanding of the dynamics of anger one can come to a constructive choice of expression.

An increased understanding of anger can help to demythologize it and, therefore, lessen its power over us. A way to do this is to trace anger to its source and examine its expression. Chart 1 (p. 21) shows this process. We will refer to it in the following discussion of the dynamics of anger.

We begin the discussion in the center of the chart (a) by defining anger as an emotion that occurs as a result of some internal or external stimuli. I run to catch a bus and the door closes just as I get there. A friend says something to me and I inwardly bristle. I wait patiently in line for the next bank teller, and someone steps in the front of the line. In these or similar situations we may find ourselves feeling angry without its being a conscious decision on our part. What has caused this feeling? Is it really the bus, the friend, the stranger that is the target of our anger? The obvious is not always the real source of anger. Generally, anger is triggered by one or all of four stimuli: frustration of a need or a want, a threat to self-esteem, injustice, and physical injury or harm (b). Of these four, physical harm or injury is the most obvious stimulant of anger and does not require explanation. Our discussions will focus on the remaining three triggers of anger.

Whenever anyone experiences one or all of the four stimuli, he or she will automatically feel angry. A person has no control over the stimuli (b) causing anger (a). Yet what is frustrating, threatening to self-esteem or unjust differs from person to person. What angers me may not anger you, because what is frustrating, threatening or unjust for me may not be the same for you. The differences in reactions to stimuli can be traced back to an individual's beliefs (c). This personal storehouse of beliefs and convictions about the inner self and the outer world determines the effect that particular stimuli will have. Thus, two people can experience the same situation and have very different reactions because their personal beliefs differ. Situations or circumstances never cause anyone's anger. The real cause of anger is found in one's beliefs. This reservoir of beliefs and convictions determines what a person will perceive as frustrating, a threat to self-esteem or an injustice. The diagram on page 22 shows this dynamic.

Chart 1

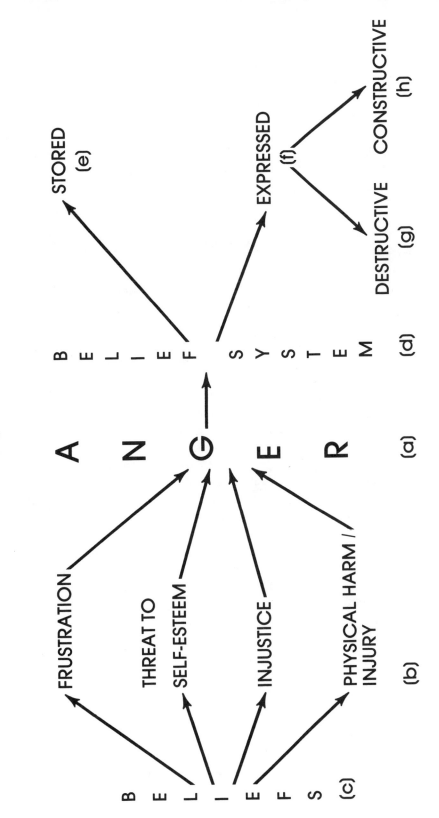

ANGER (a)

BELIEFS (d)
SYSTEM

BELIEFS (c)

FRUSTRATION

THREAT TO
SELF-ESTEEM

INJUSTICE

PHYSICAL HARM /
INJURY

(b)

STORED (e)

EXPRESSED (f)

DESTRUCTIVE (g)

CONSTRUCTIVE (h)

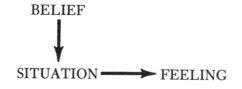

This is more clearly seen by examples.

Frustration.   Two commuters are hurrying to catch the train to take them to work. For the first person it is very important to make this particular train. He believes in keeping to a regular schedule, so it is important for him to arrive at work the same time every day. This particular day he wants to finish a project before others arrive. He prefers this train because the car is clean, he can always be assured of a seat and he enjoys the company of friends who take the same train.

The other person hurries to catch the same train. She, too, would like to take this particular one but she knows the trains are frequent and even a later one will still get her to work on time. Just as both commuters reach the platform, the train pulls away. They both have missed the train. Their reactions to this situation will be different. Given the beliefs of the first commuter, he will be very frustrated to have missed his train and will therefore feel angry. The second commuter, whose beliefs are different, will not experience the same degree of frustration. In fact, if she perceived that the train was overcrowded and the air-conditioning was not working, she may even feel relief that she missed it. While the situation is identical for both commuters, the resulting emotions are very different.

First Commuter

BELIEF: I value routine.

↓

SITUATION: misses train ⟶ FEELING: anger

Second Commuter

BELIEF: I value comfort.

↓

SITUATION: misses train ⟶ FEELING: relief

Self-esteem. An announcement of an opening for pastor is sent to the priests in a particular diocese. A number of priests apply, and two of the applicants live in the same rectory. The first priest believes that he is qualified to be a pastor. He has been a good priest for 20 years and all the parishioners love him. But he believes that the diocesan administration doesn't value him or appreciate the gifts and talents he brings to priestly ministry. He begins to think that if he isn't appointed to this position, maybe he isn't a good priest; maybe he isn't even a person of worth.

The other priest in the rectory also submits his application. Although he is happy in his present assignment, he knows that he possesses the gifts needed to be a pastor and is willing to offer those gifts to serve the diocese in this position. He sees himself as a valuable person and doesn't need the affirmation of an appointment. Though he would be happy to be pastor, it is okay if he is not chosen. His value as a person is not dependent on the appointment.

When the decision is made, neither priest is appointed pastor. Their reactions will differ drastically. The first priest will be angry, seeing his not being appointed as an attack on his self-esteem. Because he was not chosen, he feels that no one at the diocesan office appreciates him. He is angry that they do not see him as qualified to be a pastor. He decides that if they think so little of him, he will never apply for another pastorate. The other priest will react differently. Perhaps he thinks he has different gifts than are needed for that particular parish. He had heard that the parish was in financial difficulty and the new pastor needed to be skilled in fundraising. He knows his gifts are more people-oriented, so he feels that it is probably just as well that he was not chosen. He is hopeful that the future will offer a parish more suited to his qualifications.

While neither priest was selected as pastor, the difference in their reactions lies in the area of each one's personal beliefs. For the first priest the beliefs he holds about himself and others are such that the rejection is an affront to his self-esteem. This triggers anger. While the rejection is the same for the second priest, his beliefs do not lead him to feel threatened.

First Priest

BELIEF: I'm only of value if I am chosen pastor.

↓

SITUATION: He is not appointed pastor. ——→ FEELING: anger

Second Priest

BELIEF: I'm of value for who I am.

↓

SITUATION: He is not appointed ——→ FEELING: indifference
            pastor.

Injustice.   Four sisters have applied to their congregation's administration for the use of a car for the coming year. Two sisters receive positive responses while the other two receive a refusal with no explanation. One of the two refused receives her letter and she is disappointed, but she figures that maybe there aren't enough cars to go around, or maybe her need for a car is not as great as another's, or maybe the requests are answered on a first-come, first-served basis. She decides that she will try again next term.

The other sister who receives a negative letter "hits the roof." She believes that after giving 30 years to her community and laboring in the community apostolate, she deserves a positive response to any request she makes. Certainly she deserves a response for as simple or as necessary a request as this one. Besides she thinks the provincial administrator doesn't like her and may even be jealous of her. She feels she has been treated unfairly and complains about her mistreatment to anyone who will listen.

Both sisters received the same letter denying their request, yet their responses to the letters are remarkably different. Again, we see that the differences lie not in the situation, but in the individual's set of beliefs and convictions.

First Sister

BELIEF: The provincial treats everyone equitably.

↓

SITUATION: Sister is refused car. ➤ FEELING: acceptance

Second Sister

BELIEF: The provincial does not treat me fairly.

↓

SITUATION: Sister is refused car. ➤ FEELING: anger

As the above examples illustrate, whenever I experience what I personally consider an injustice, frustration or a threat to self-esteem, I will automatically feel angry. In order to change the feeling of anger that I am experiencing, I will have to change the beliefs that are causing the feeling. Feelings follow beliefs. Only when I decide to change a belief will the subsequent feeling also change. As you reflect on a personal experience of anger, can you move past the situation that is the trigger and identify the belief that is the real cause of your anger? Is this a belief that is life-giving and growth-producing for you? Or is it a belief that you would wish to change? For example:

ORIGINAL BELIEF: I need to be perfect in all things.

↓

SITUATION: I make a mistake. ➤ FEELING: anger

CHANGED BELIEF: I'm not less a person when I fail.

↓

SITUATION: I make a mistake. ➤ FEELING: acceptance

There are times in all our lives when we experience frustration, a threat to self-esteem and injustice simultaneously, and the feeling of anger multiplied is rage. Let us imagine three people attending the same Sunday liturgy. In one of the pews is a parishioner who is frustrated because the changes in the church took away some favorite devotions. He feels he is not valued because he is a lay person and sees the church unjust in its lack of support of the poor in the area.

In another pew sits a woman religious. Watching the priest at the altar reminds her that because she is a woman, she is prevented from using her gifts to the fullest in the church. She feels frustrated and devalued as a person. She also believes that the church's attitude toward women is unjust.

At the altar is a priest. The laity and religious in his parish blame him for anything they don't like about the church and this threatens his self-esteem. He would like to spend most of his time with his parishioners, but he is frustrated that he is occupied by dealing with so many building concerns and financial details, for which he has had little training. On top of this, he believes that his appointment to this parish was an arbitrary decision, and sees the diocesan placement policy as unjust and insensitive.

Each of the three experiences frustration, an attack on self-esteem and an injustice. Each one feels rage, but for different reasons.

The rage of the three people at the liturgy stems from a set of personal beliefs that are important and life-giving for them. Although beliefs and convictions are areas over which we have control, we do not always choose to change our beliefs. This is especially true for those convictions that give meaning and direction to our life. There are other beliefs that each one of us holds about ourselves, others and life that are not life-giving. For example, I may believe that I should be perfect in all things. Given this belief I may find myself continually frustrated and, therefore, angry. Realizing the effect this belief has on my emotional life may move me to decide to change this belief. On the other hand, I may believe that every human person deserves respect and dignity. Whenever I see a violation of this belief, I will feel angry. Given this belief, I cannot control feeling the anger. Even though I cannot control feeling an emotion, I always have the power to exercise free will as to whether or not I will act upon that emotion.

Let us summarize what has been said so far on the first side of the chart:

Whenever I feel angry, do I:

1. Acknowledge and accept the feeling of anger?

2. Find what has triggered the angry feeling?
   (Is there something I want or need that has been frustrated? Is there some threat to my self-esteem? Do I feel wronged in some way? Are all three areas involved?)

3. Identify the beliefs about my self, others, life that are causing the anger?

4. Decide whether these are beliefs I want to maintain or to change?

5. Choose how I will express this anger?

This fifth step moves into the expression of anger and to the other side of the chart.

Anger is a form of energy and, following a general principle of science, we know that energy can only be changed, not destroyed. Energy can be defined as the power to do work. We choose the work toward which this energy is directed. But how we choose to express our anger is related to the beliefs we hold about it. The energy created from feeling angry must pass through our belief system (see Chart 2, p. 28). *I* determine how the energy created by anger will be changed and released.

Belief System (d)

Each of us has a system of beliefs about anger as an emotion. These beliefs were initially formed in childhood. At some point in life people look at what they have learned in childhood to see if it is growth-producing and beneficial or if it is life-zapping and destructive. This is true for beliefs about anger as well as other beliefs, attitudes and values. As adults, people may choose to keep belief systems about anger intact or they can choose to change them. Before either choice can be made, however, a person has to raise those beliefs to consciousness and critically analyze them. This system of beliefs is a motivating force for behavior. When a person's belief system holds anger as a negative emotion, anger will be denied and the energy created by anger will be stored (e). If the system of beliefs holds anger as a positive emotion, then the energy of anger will be expressed in some way (f).

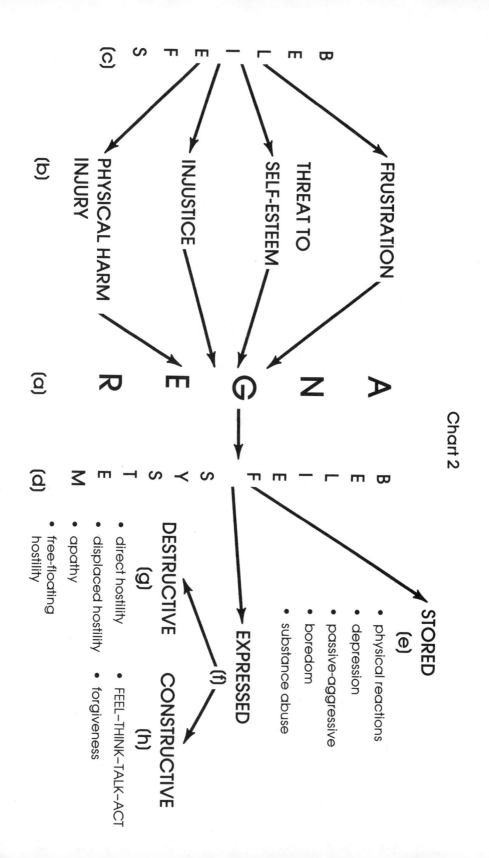

Chart 2

The negative beliefs (conscious or unconscious) about anger as an emotion may sound like this:

— Good people (Christians) do not get angry.

— There should be peace at any price.

— Anger always leads to destructive actions.

— Anger is likely to hurt someone.

— Holy people do not feel angry.

— Anger is sinful.

Stored Anger (e)

When the belief system brands anger as a negative emotion, people will work hard to deny that feeling. One can push down the feeling (suppression) or not allow the feeling into consciousness (repression). Persons for whom anger is a negative emotion may try to hide or store those feelings not only from others, but especially from themselves. There is energy created by anger, however, and that energy has to have an outlet. Anger that is continually stored is a destructive option. It has serious consequences in that it destroys both the person and relationships. Stored anger will have internal reactions and will affect the person physiologically as well as psychologically. Stored anger can assume a number of faces: It can cause physical reactions, function as an explosive pressure cooker, cause depression, mask itself in expressions that appear more personally and socially acceptable, inspire communication through passive-aggressive behavior or anesthetize feeling.

Physical reaction.   Whenever a person feels angry, a physical reaction is present. For some the face reddens, blood pressure and pulse rate increase, the epinephrine (adrenaline) level rises. The body moves into an excited state. It anticipates a threat and readies itself for protection. The body prepares for a fight/flight reaction.

When the mind receives the message that anger is being experienced, it in turn sends a message to the glands within the body. These glands begin producing such necessary hormones as ACTH, epinephrine, norepinephrine and cortisone. Each one of these is important for the body, but in excessive doses they prove harmful. They can be compared to cholesterol. The body produces and needs cholesterol; excessive levels of cholesterol, however, are counterproductive. When the psyche is trying to deny the existence of anger, the body does not receive the message and continues to overproduce these hormones. People who adopt a perennial attitude of denial are constantly allowing their bodies to build up to a physically excited state. This will result in a variety of illnesses, such as heart attack, stroke, ulcers and high blood pressure. In this case, stored anger can actually kill you.

Stored anger carries with it other consequences. Each time anger is triggered, it is denied and pushed inward. Picture a pressure cooker into which is poured all unacceptable emotions. The problem is that the pressure cooker has a certain capacity. At some point, as the heat is turned up, the cover will blow. The person explodes at the wrong time, in the wrong place, to the wrong person, with the wrong intensity. For instance, a staff person who is expert in denying and storing anger walks into the parish office. The secretary has typed a letter for the person but it contains a minor mistake. The staff person rants and raves at the secretary for this insignificant error. This explosion, however, leaves the staff person feeling guilty because it goes against a belief that a good person does not get angry. The person's self-esteem is then lowered and in turn produces anger, which continues the destructive cycle. The person feels frustrated and angry but the belief system does not permit expression, so the anger is again stored. The cycle is repeated over and over again. This form of expression plays havoc not only with self-esteem but also with relationships.

Depression.   One of the greatest causes of depression is anger turned inward. Depression can have many causes. There are 24 diseases known to directly produce depression.[3] In addition, depression can result from significant losses, chemical imbalance, nutritional deficiencies, or personal crisis, especially repeated crises. From our experience of counseling people in ministry, depression emerges as the major presenting problem (though it is often masked).

There is an interesting, but destructive, logic at work in the lives of many religiously oriented people (especially full-time ministers). The unconscious logic follows this path: Anger is bad, maybe even sinful, but depression is not sinful or bad. Therefore, it is better (I am a better person) when I am depressed rather than angry. For these individuals, the anger is stored. It is usually directed toward self (often blaming self) and results in the painful, devastating and paralyzing experience of depression.

Anger converted to an acceptable emotion. Anger can also be temporarily stored, then converted to a more acceptable emotion. For instance, anger may be expressed as boredom. It is a state of dissatisfaction and a disinclination to act. Boredom is masked anger. Let us take an example of a parishioner who inwardly seethes through the Sunday homily and later complains to friends about how boring it was. The parishioner may feel frustrated and therefore angry that the church is not responding to contemporary world needs. Anger, however, is not an acceptable emotion for this person, so it is converted to a more socially acceptable one—boredom. Such transference never allows the person to experience the real emotion of anger and to decide how to express it constructively.

The fear of anger can also take another form of behavior, for example, *passive aggression*. Passive-aggressive people cannot admit feelings of anger and they behave in such a way that they effectively trigger frustration in another, usually not by what they do but by what they do not do. Their omission produces frustration in the other and the frustrated person may act out the anger of the passive-aggressive. This allows a passive-aggressive person to maintain denial of the emotion.

One example of such behavior is a teacher who is angry at a certain administrative decision of the department chairperson. For this teacher, anger is a negative emotion. Because of this belief system, the teacher cannot feel or express the anger. Instead, the teacher submits all her reports late. The chairperson, who must receive these reports by a certain date, becomes frustrated, feels angry and expresses that anger. The passive-aggressive can observe and judge the anger of the other, and pity a person who feels and acts angry, which, of course, the passive-aggressive never does. Willard Gaylin describes passive-aggressive behavior as "assault by indirection and disguise."[4] It is not uncommon for people who find it difficult to accept and express anger to rely on passive-aggressive behavior.

Substance abuse and sexual acting out are also ways of denying anger by *anesthetizing the feeling*. There is an underlying belief that these behaviors will prevent the person from having to admit and deal with feelings of anger. It is apparent that these are self-destructive.

Sarcasm and withdrawal are other behaviors that serve the purpose of defending a person from feeling anger. While they may appear to protect the individual temporarily, the anger remains hidden within. Emotions do not remain permanently stifled and eventually all emotions find expression, sometimes in indirect or unconscious ways.

To summarize, anger is experienced when some internal or external stimuli frustrates, threatens self-esteem or is unjust, and is in contradiction to a person's beliefs about self and life. The energy of anger is channeled through the system of beliefs that one holds about anger. Depending on the beliefs, anger can be denied existence and stored in differing ways or anger can be expressed. Anger, when believed to be a negative emotion, is stored.

Expressed Anger (f)

An individual's system of beliefs may hold anger as a positive and acceptable emotion. These beliefs will allow the individual to become aware of and experience the feeling of anger. The conscious or unconscious beliefs about anger as a positive emotion might sound like this:

— Anger is a normal emotion, like any other emotion.

— It is okay to feel angry.

— Anger does not have to lead to destructive actions.

— I'm a good person even when I feel angry.

— Anger is not sinful.

These and similar beliefs free a person to express the anger when it is experienced. Not all expressions of anger, however, are life-giving; anger can be expressed destructively as well as constructively. Every person could probably relate a time when something or someone sparked anger and one immediately reacted without thinking, only later to regret that action. The person is not bad because anger is expressed destructively, nor are destructive expressions of anger always intentional. An ever-expanding understanding of the dynamics of anger can help one to choose behavior that is growth-producing and life-giving for oneself and others.

Destructive Anger (g)   Hostility is one of the most destructive ways of expressing anger. Webster defines hostility as an act of open enmity. While anger is an emotion, hostility is an act, a behavior that treats another with ill will and malevolence. Hostility breeds hostility. When I experience hostility from another, I usually become hostile in return. Hostility is contagious. It destroys family, ministry and community. Hostility is behavior that treats another as an enemy who must be attacked or destroyed. Hostility can take four forms: direct, displaced, apathetic and free-floating.

1. *Direct hostility.*   As we noted before, there are normally three triggers of anger: frustration, threat to self-esteem and injustice. When someone believes that another person is the cause of anger, he or she may blame the other and react accordingly. The man in our earlier example who missed the train may blame his neighbor, who asked him a question as he was leaving the house. When he returns home that night, if the neighbor stops him to chat, he might respond hostilely. This is an example of direct hostility. The animosity is expressed directly toward the person who is considered the cause of the anger. As noted earlier, however, no one can make us angry; emotions are produced by our beliefs.

2. *Displaced hostility.*   If the person who is thought to be the cause of anger is someone in a position of authority, or is seen as too threatening, a person may transfer hostility to a less dangerous person or even to an inanimate object. Several years ago a cartoon appeared in a local paper that is a good example of displaced hostility. A woman returns home from a very difficult day at work. She is angry because her boss has given her an evaluation she considers unfair. She, therefore, is angry but fears that any response on her part will hinder future promotion. That evening, for no apparent reason, she becomes hostile toward her husband. Because he senses their relationship is not on firm ground, he is afraid to react to his wife's hostility. However, when their child asks to visit a friend's house the father shouts at the child. The child is angry at both parents but is afraid to show that anger for fear of punishment. The child goes up to a bedroom and kicks the dog sitting at the door. Hostility can have a chain effect. In each case there has been hostility displaced onto something or someone that is considered safer.

3. *Apathetic hostility.*   The relationship between apathy and hostility is less obvious. Some may even consider it virtuous to

adopt a stance of "live and let live." They might even say, "Doesn't the Bible say, 'Am I my brother's keeper?' "

A psychiatrist was conducting a workshop when someone stated a philosophy of live and let live. He quickly retorted, "You mean live and let die!" He then went on to describe a typical scene in Christian communities and among ministry groups: Members of the community or staff are emotionally or spiritually dying while the rest of the group remains on the periphery, not wanting to become involved in the pain of others. Their apathy is actually a form of hostility.

The disease of alcoholism can also give rise to apathetic behavior. When a member of a family, staff or community is suffering from alcoholism, the other members can too easily hide behind the excuse of not wanting to interfere. Yet this excuse can be masking fear of confrontation or fear of the victim's anger that could result. The absence of involvement condemns the victim to a slow process of dying. Their choice of non-involvement is hostile behavior.

The deleterious effects of apathy are pronounced in the example of the millions of Jews and Polish Catholics massacred during the Second World War while others stood by and did nothing to prevent these atrocities. Many Christian communities today are sinning by apathetically turning their collective backs on the countless millions of poor and suffering, finding comfort and justification in turning all their energy toward more internal church, parish or community issues. In his encyclical on social concerns, Pope John Paul II writes that "The Church is . . . obliged by her vocation—she herself, her ministers and each of her members—to relieve the misery of the suffering, both far and near, not only out of her 'abundance,' but out of her 'necessities.' Faced by cases of need, one cannot ignore them in favor of superfluous church ornaments and costly furnishings for divine worship; on the contrary, it could be obligatory to sell these goods in order to provide food, drink, clothing and shelter for those who need these things."[5] Yet in almost every Christian parish there is an inordinate amount of energy directed toward liturgy with little or none toward galvanizing the community to pool its resources of people, money, energy and time to respond to the poor. The Notre Dame study on parish life states that less than two percent of core Catholics are involved in social action activities.[6]

In contrast to this, we know of a parish that sponsored a parish fair that raised about $125,000. Not one penny of the collected amount was returned to the parish. All the money raised was sent to projects to feed the poor. This is the opposite of apathy.

4. *Free-floating hostility.*   There are people whose norm of behavior is to attack anyone and everyone over any issue at any time. This can be the behavior of those whose inner beliefs about self are so unrealistic as to continually set them up for failure and frustration. In addition, self-esteem is at a low level and the only way to bolster self is to put others down. Others may see this type of person as an "angry person" but he or she is really a hurting person. Hostile behavior provides an inpenetrable shield that defends one from human interactions, preventing both hurt and life-giving relationships. It is evident that when people have low self-esteem, they display a high degree of hostility and competitiveness. The reverse is also true. People who have high self-esteem display a low degree of hostility and competitiveness.

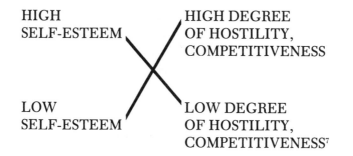

HIGH SELF-ESTEEM

HIGH DEGREE OF HOSTILITY, COMPETITIVENESS

LOW SELF-ESTEEM

LOW DEGREE OF HOSTILITY, COMPETITIVENESS[7]

Constructive Anger (h)   Each of us has beliefs and convictions that give meaning and direction to life, and we do not choose to change them. For example, I may strongly believe that every human person is a child of God. Whenever I see religious rights violated, I will feel angry. Because I hold this belief, I cannot control feeling this emotion. Feeling angry does not mean that I will automatically act on that feeling without any control over how I will act. We can choose to express the energy produced by anger creatively and constructively.

If the experience of anger puts me in an excited state, then the first step is to move into a calm state. Only when I am calm am I free to make a wise decision about how I will express the anger I am currently experiencing. There are a variety of methods that can be employed. For some it will be jogging or exercise; for others it can be music, meditation, centering, deep breathing. Each person has to determine what will be most helpful in bringing about a feeling of calm and relaxation. From your own experience of anger, what has proved beneficial for you?

Becoming calm, however, is not the primary goal; it is only a means to an end. The aim is to direct the energy constructively, not to dissipate it. Our belief is that anger is most constructive when it is moved from the heart, where the emotion is felt, to the head where some clarity emerges before it comes out the mouth.[8] When people feel angry, they generally don't think clearly, speak rationally or feel compassionately—the three qualities necessary to deal constructively with anger. When one experiences anger, there is a spontaneous tendency to act out that feeling. Because anger places a person in an emotionally aroused state and the reasoning process is cloudy, precipitous actions can have harmful repercussions.

A simple four-step process can be helpful in moving a person from feeling to action that can be more growth-producing and life-giving. We present this paradigm and suggest that, when used, it is a constructive method for handling anger. Refer back to your own personal example of anger and see how the paradigm might have changed your initial response to the situation.

Anger Paradigm:

Feel ⟶ Think ⟶ Talk ⟶ Act

Feel. Allow yourself to feel angry. This is especially important if your first reaction is to deny the feeling. What is the intensity of the anger? Annoyed? Miffed? Furious? Enraged? Labeling the intensity of the emotion initially may prove helpful as you move through the paradigm and decide upon a course of action. Do you accept the feeling as a normal, human emotion? Can you own the feeling or do you blame another for the feeling you experience?

There are two major problems at this initial step. First, I may simply experience the feeling of anger and skip over the middle two steps, thus short-circuiting the process. When this occurs, the result is almost always destructive to self, relationships, ministry or community.

Secondly, if I don't initially experience and admit to feeling angry, the next two steps will not occur. When this is the case, the anger frequently comes out indirectly. At a social gathering, for instance, harsh words transpire between two people. The first person attempts to talk about the exchange, but the other claims there was no feeling involved and no need to pursue the issue. Within the hour, with other people gathered around, the second person makes a sarcastic remark about the first person. Not only was the speaker unaware of the feeling, but also that the remark was a hostile expression of that feeling.

For some individuals, feelings of anger have been blocked from their awareness and there may be something that prevents them from simply tapping into the feeling. These individuals may find the need for professional assistance to help them get in touch with their feelings of anger.

Given the fact that getting in touch with feelings is often difficult for people in ministry, this may well be the most important step to take.[9] It is not always possible to admit certain feelings immediately. Building a structure into one's day that forces a review of events and responses can facilitate this process. Different methods, such as a "consciousness examen," will be helpful.[10]

Think.   In order to avoid acting precipitously upon an angry feeling, move into a calm state that will allow you to think more clearly. Pausing a few moments (whatever length of time is needed) provides the opportunity for some important exploration. This quiet, reflective time should be used to:

1.   Identify the cause of the anger: What has triggered the feeling? What belief is the real cause of the anger?

2.   Rate its importance: not everything that triggers anger is of equal importance. This is where labeling the intensity of the anger may prove helpful. Am I annoyed because someone left dirty dishes in the sink and it frustrates my belief that things should be neat and tidy? Or am I enraged because I experienced an affront to human respect and my belief in human dignity has been violated? Whereas in both situations I may feel angry, the two situations are not equal in importance and the resulting response will vary because of that difference. If the emotional reaction is out of proportion to the situation,

then the real cause of the anger may still be unidentified. Rating the situation and cause of the anger will help chart a realistic course of action.

3.   Purify motives. The desire for revenge may be the primary, though unconscious, reaction to anger. Calm reflection can help us move past this primitive reflex. Motive should serve as the pivotal point for any action or reaction we might take. For example, if I am angry at a friend's comment, do I convey my hurt to the friend because the friendship is important or because I want to get even?

Sometimes it is difficult to achieve calm in the midst of the situation. Simply asking for a couple of minutes to calm down, or even excusing yourself for a few minutes, can provide breathing space for both parties and prevent precipitous action that might later be regretted. In a group setting, taking time to become calm is also recommended. If need be and if it is possible, temporarily remove yourself from the situation. At a recent meeting, one of us felt anger rising and, fearing it would be converted to hostility, suggested a 15-minute break. The time was given for all involved to think and reflect, thereby allowing everyone to calm down. This thinking time prevented the anger from being converted to hostility.

It may not always be possible to leave a situation long enough to become calm, so alternative coping methods can be employed. The key idea is to find some way to calm down in order to think logically about the cause of the anger. Taking several deep breaths can relax the bodily manifestations of anger. The age-old suggestion of pausing to count to ten can also be effective in lessening the volatility of the moment. At a formal gathering, such as a meeting, some people find that doodling or writing serves to release pent up emotions and helps them to respond more rationally.

When it is possible to leave the situation, use the time away to try to identify the real cause of the feeling by tracing the path of anger (refer to chart 1, p. 21). Label what has triggered the emotion. Is there something that I want or need in this situation that is being frustrated? Do I feel attacked or is my self-esteem being threatened in some way? Do I see injustice here, or do I feel wronged or injured? Once the triggers of the feeling are discovered, then the area of beliefs can be examined. What is the personal belief that is at the root of the anger? Is this belief important to who I am as a person? Is the belief life-giving and growth-producing? Is this belief affected by how I perceive myself or others? Do I choose to assess those perceptions?

Exploring beliefs can help to rate the importance of the incident. Not all that angers us is of equal importance. Thinking allows the opportunity to purify one's motives, especially if further communication is intended. Do I want to communicate with another to convey how I feel, or do I simply want to retaliate?

Talk. The initial reaction following anger is revenge. Therefore, immediately talking to the person with whom I'm in conflict may merely serve to ignite the fire. Sometimes our perceptions of a situation cloud our ability to see the situation from the other side and leave us unable to move past our initial reaction. The purpose of this step is to seek help in sorting out the experience.

Given the purpose, the person I look to for help should be someone who can be objective, not merely sympathetic. Someone who only reinforces the feeling will not be helpful: "I understand how angry you are. Do you know what he or she did to me?" The objective person can be a friend, family member, colleague or any person who can help me answer questions and challenge me to further self-knowledge and growth. The aim of this step is to talk to someone to help me sort out and reflect on questions such as: Why are my feelings so intense over this incident? What has triggered my angry feelings? Are my perceptions of myself distorting my perception of the incident? What are my perceptions of the other? What is the belief that is at the root of my anger? What is the best course of action for me to take? The goal of the listener is to help you gain insight and choose actions that will be constructive.

Act. Exploring possibilities for constructively dealing with the anger can take different avenues. It is in choice of expression that one exercises control and free will. One choice of action may be to return to the person and state your feelings. Dialogue at this juncture can be productive, because there has been time to reflect and think.

Another avenue can be to change the beliefs that are the source of the anger. For example, if the cause of anger is a belief that I must be perfect, changing that belief will allow me to fail without becoming angry.

Another constructive expression of anger can be to channel the energy into another source. For example, when I feel angry over the unresponsiveness of municipal government to the plight of the homeless, I can channel that energy into investigating or changing the unjust situation. In addition, the energy engendered by anger can also be used for creative outlets, such as music and art.

Finally, we recommend forgiveness as a preferred constructive expression of anger for Christians. Because Chapter 3 will be devoted to this topic, we will simply mention it here as a constructive expression of anger.

Recount all the specifics of the situation that caused you to feel angry. What triggered your anger? How did you express that anger? Can you identify the cause of your anger? If the same situation were to occur today, what, if anything, would you do differently?

Summary of steps to take in dealing with anger

1. Acknowledge and accept the feeling of anger that you are presently experiencing. Allow yourself to experience the anger, labeling the intensity of the emotion.

2. Become calm. What can I do right now to calm myself so I can begin to think through the situation?

3. Try to identify the need, want, attack on self-esteem or injustice that has stimulated the anger. Try to move past the trigger and identify the belief(s) or conviction(s) that is really causing the anger.

4. Determine how essential for me is the belief at issue.

5. Decide what action I want to take to express my anger:
    —Look at the situation itself. How would I rate its importance in my life?
    —Is this situation of enough consequence that I need assistance in working through my feelings?
    —What is my motive in expressing my feelings? What do I hope to achieve by expressing them?
    —Are my perceptions of the situation distorted?

6. Look at the situation and the individuals involved when deciding upon the most appropriate action.

   —Do I want to return to the person(s) and state my feelings?

   —Do I want to initiate another action that would be more suitable, given the cause of the anger?

   —Do I want to channel my energy into a creative outlet?

   —Do I choose to change my belief that caused the anger?

7. Decide to forgive.

Notes

[1] Jane E. Brody, *New York Times*, March, 1983.

[2] Hans Selye, *Stress Without Distress* (New York: Signet, 1974).

[3] *Human Development*, Vol. 6, no. 1, Spring, 1985, p. 19.

[4] Willard Gaylin, *The Rage Within*, p. 104.

[5] Pope John Paul II, Encyclical Letter, *The Social Concerns of the Church*.

[6] David Leege and Thomas A. Trozzolo, "Participation in Catholic Parish Life: Religious Rite and Parish Activities in the 1980s" *Notre Dame Study on Catholic Parish Life*, University of Notre Dame, Report No. 3, April, 1985.

[7] Linda Amadeo, R.N., M.S., and James Gill, S.J., M.D., "Managing Anger, Hostility and Aggression," *Human Development*, Vol. I, no. 3, Fall, 1980, p. 44. A more comprehensive discussion of free-floating hostility can be found in an article by James Gill, S.J., "Indispensable Self-Esteem," *Human Development*, Vol. I, No. 3, Fall, 1980.

[8] Loughlan Sofield, S.T. and Carroll Juliano, S.H.C.J., *Collaborative Ministry: Skills and Guidelines* (Notre Dame, IN: Ave Maria Press, 1987), pp. 113ff.

[9] National Opinion Research Center, *The Catholic Priest in the United States: Sociological Investigations* (Washington, D.C.: United States Catholic Conference, 1972).

[10] George Aschenbrenner, S.J., "Consciousness Examen," *Review for Religious*, Vol. 31, January, 1972, pp. 14-21.

Chapter Two

Anger: A Case Study

In Chapter 1 we traced the emotion of anger from its inception to expression, delineating the normal dynamics involved. This chapter gives life to those dynamics. After relating a true incident, we will identify and develop some general principles about anger.

Let us introduce a scenario that could happen to any of us. The following story was related during a workshop when the topic of anger was introduced. The incident involved two women religious who were close friends. They were enjoying the day together when the sister who was relating the story offered some advice to her friend as part of their conversation. She was quite taken aback to hear her friend shout, "You're always correcting me. You make me feel terrible." Unable to respond to what she felt was an unjust condemnation, the sister darted out the door, slamming it behind her. She told the workshop participants, "I felt and acted like a four year old."

Following the incident, she had retreated to her room feeling angry. "I hated her," she declared. "I was so angry with her, I could have killed her." She remained in her room for two hours pondering the incident, feeding on her anger, justifying her own behavior, practicing sharp, hostile remarks to say to her friend, and telling herself that it was all her friend's fault. She convinced herself she was totally in the right and had been wronged by her friend.

After a couple of hours of creating this devastating dialogue in her mind, she reluctantly began to recall some of the beautiful times they had shared together as friends. The image of the good times slowly melted the anger. The hostility she had nurtured during the last few hours diminished. She spent time sorting through her feelings and thinking about what she really wanted to happen. Their friendship was something very dear to her and one of the greatest gifts in her life. She thought about her next step and began to explore some options. Her decision was a simple one. She approached her friend and asked, "What's happening between us? Do you want to talk about it?"

Her friend explained the insecurity she was feeling in her job, and that the comment only accentuated that feeling. The other sister responded that she felt devalued when her suggestion met with a sharp rebuff. Fortunately, both women were willing to risk and openly discuss their feelings about the encounter. They both knew honest dialogue made them more vulnerable to hurt, but the importance of the relationship in their lives outweighed the risk. They listened and shared. In retelling her story, the sister described their final sharing as a sacramental moment. As a result of the encounter their friendship was deepened.

What can we learn from this case study concerning anger? In the following pages we will use the incident to develop some general principles about anger. We invite readers to think about the general principles in light of how they apply in their own experience.

It will be worthwhile to keep several questions in mind while reading this chapter.

—Do I agree with the principle presented?

—How is this principle evidenced in my own life?

—How can my understanding of this principle help me in my family, work, ministry and community?

Basic Principles

1. Anger is a normal aspect of all relationships.
2. Anger is a complex emotion.
3. Perception colors our view of reality and triggers anger.
4. Imagery plays a major role in intensifying or defusing anger.
5. Anger may be more difficult for those who are religiously oriented.

6. Anger often fosters regression.

7. Anger is usually a precondition for conflict.

8. Anger and conflict are generally related to basic human needs.

9. Most people have the capacity to work through anger and conflict.

10. Anger and conflict can produce growth.

11. For Christians the ultimate goal of anger and conflict is forgiveness.

Anger as a Normal Emotion

As the sister related her story she seemed genuinely surprised that she could become *so* angry toward someone for whom she cared so deeply. Perhaps people are more comfortable feeling angry toward someone they don't like or don't know. It may be more difficult to become angry toward someone one cares about or relates to personally or professionally. Whenever two or more people interact, the emotion of anger will inevitably appear at many points in the relationship.

As was pointed out in Chapter 1, anger is an automatic reaction to frustration, an attack on self-esteem, an injustice or physical harm. Anger will not have a paralyzing effect on a person when there is an understanding of the dynamics of anger and an acceptance of it as a normal emotion that is part of all relationships. As the sister related the incident, it was evident to all listening that she could accept her feelings of anger and was quite in touch with the degree of intensity she was experiencing. Rather than berate herself for the anger she felt, she began to sort out her feelings.

Unfortunately, for many people this is not the case. As we already noted, the belief, conscious or unconscious, that anger and conflict should not exist among Christians is at work in many lives. This belief about anger will lead a person to deny the presence of feeling, and this can have disastrous consequences. For some the emotion of anger has moral overtones—it is "sinful" to feel angry. While most people would deny this statement on the intellectual level, the belief is a dominant factor in the emotional life and behavior of many.

To the extent that we can accept anger as a natural, healthy, human emotion and one without moral overtones, we can more readily accept it in ourselves and in relationships. Feelings of anger, recognized and expressed constructively, can be opportunities for growth within the individual and between individuals. This is apparent in the case study above. The experience of anger became life-giving for both parties.

Do I accept anger as a normal emotion, as I would joy, love or hate? What are my beliefs about anger that might make it difficult to admit the presence of this emotion? Am I surprised when I experience anger in my family, friendships, ministry, community?

Anger as a Complex Emotion

Anger is one of the more complex emotions. Feelings and emotions, in and of themselves, are neither good nor bad. Each person is responsible for adding the negative or positive note to certain emotions and feelings. For example, emotions such as love and joy may be seen as positive and acceptable emotions, whereas emotions such as anger, sadness and fear may be considered as negative and therefore not acceptable. In his book *The Rage Within*, Willard Gaylin defines anger as "essentially a basic emotional response to stress which alerts, motivates and invigorates the organism to defend its basic interests." Emotions are bodily and affective reactions to stimuli. These stimuli can be internal (beliefs, perceptions, images) or external (people, situations, physical threats).

Viewed from this perspective, anger takes on a connotation drastically different from that usually ascribed to it. First, it is a warning device, alerting the person to something important happening. Do you respond to this intrapsychic warning system in the same way you would to a smoke detector warning the presence of a fire? The warning should provide the impetus to search for the cause and to prevent destruction. Too often a person's unconscious mechanism, hearing anger's warning system, simply tries to ignore or run away from it.

How do you take advantage of the motivational aspect of anger? Left to its own devices, anger will motivate to self-defense or an inappropriate and inadequate reaction. Ultimately anger should motivate a person to action, but not a blind, undisciplined, unreflected action, but rather an action chosen because of its positive effect on personal, relational, communal and ministerial growth and goals. When anger motivates a person to a spontaneous, unreflected action, it is often more destructive than constructive.

Anger is instrinsically invigorating and potentially life-giving, though it is often perceived as the opposite. An individual who experiences anger determines whether it will be life- or death-producing. When anger is viewed as a positive, life-giving, potentially creative force, one's response to anger will become less defensive. Anger's potential to be life-giving will be realized.

Emotions can be either painful (sadness) or pleasant (joy). Normally speaking, anger is an extremely unpleasant and painful emotion. In many instances anger is experienced with a strong intensity, although that may not always be the case. For example, if you drop and break a crystal vase, you may feel annoyed or upset at your carelessness. But when a person experiences anger in interpersonal relationships, the feeling is usually of much greater intensity. In the case study the sisters experienced very intense feelings of anger. Not everyone can accept intense feelings in themselves or in others. Some are frightened by their feelings, especially those of anger. As a result, when they experience a situation that triggers an intense feeling of anger, they are reluctant to admit the intensity of that emotion. They find it more comfortable to admit "feeling a little annoyed" or some other mild expression of anger, rather than recognize the rage that may be seething just below the surface. This person would be unable to admit, let alone verbalize, the powerful feelings as described by the sister in the case study.

Rarely do our emotions exist singly. One frequently experiences many emotions simultaneously and it is not always easy to sort out those feelings. An inability to admit the degree or feeling of anger may stem from the fact that anger can trigger within us other emotions, such as fear, anxiety and guilt. The specific emotions triggered by anger depend on how a person's individual background and personal history taught one to view anger. Children who see physical violence between parents as a result of anger, for example, may as adults feel fear whenever they are angry or see another angry. They fear both being harmed and harming others. Adults who as children saw anger considered as a normal emotion are more disposed to express anger in a constructive way.

Most of us can identify the relationship between fear and anger. Take the situation of driving along a highway at high speed.

Another car suddenly cuts in front of you and you must hit the brakes in order to avoid an accident. In that split second you will most likely experience a jumble of emotions. Probably the predominant emotion you identify is fear, for your own life and the lives of others. Then a feeling of anger at the carelessness or stupidity of the other driver takes over and is mixed with a feeling of relief and a desire for revenge.

There is a two-way relationship between anger and fear. First, there is the fear of one's own anger. We refer here to an irrational fear that anger is, and will always be, destructive. Secondly, there is the fear of the anger of others. Fear of anger can paralyze an individual or a group. In community or ministry groups those members who express anger are often allowed to control the group. The more their anger is expressed in a juvenile, almost primitive fashion, the more the group fears them and relinquishes control. Have you experienced a time when one person, whose behavior was explosive, seemed to control everyone else? What feelings did you experience at that time? How do you usually respond to a person in this type of situation? It is our belief that the ultimate problem is not the person expressing the anger, but the fear and passivity of those who because of fear allow and encourage this immature behavior.

Besides fear, there is also the issue of anxiety. Anxiety is an emotion produced when there is ambiguity or lack of clarity about the source of the fear. In the above example of the near car crash, the emotion was fear. We knew the source of the emotion. Our imagery conveys clearly what might have occurred if the two cars collided. We could picture the destruction and that image produces fear. With the fear comes all the physical symptoms: rapid breath, sweating, increased heart rate, and so forth. There are times when we experience the same emotion but the source is not clear. Perhaps we awake some morning feeling all these symptoms for no reason. This is anxiety: The object of what we fear is not clear.

Anger and Perceptions

A friend related a story. "When I awoke one morning, I wasn't feeling particularly good about myself. I had just finished a workshop and I wasn't pleased with how it went. As I dressed my skirt was a little snug. Weight is an area of great sensitivity for me and that morning I was feeling fat. Although I had fixed my hair, even it didn't look right. Basically, I was pretty down on myself.

"I thought that I had placed my feelings aside as I left for work. On entering the office I spotted a colleague from another branch whom I met several years ago. Since that time our paths had not crossed. She was a woman who exerted great influence on our boss and it was important to me that I make a good impression on her.

"We greeted each other. I reintroduced myself, adding that I was not sure she remembered me. 'Of course, I do,' she replied and then added, 'Oh my, haven't you lost weight. You look so trim!' Her words sent me into a tailspin of emotions and self-talk. I mumbled some incoherent sentences to her and returned to my office. My internal ramblings went like this: 'Lost weight! My heaven, I feel like a beached whale! If she thinks I look trim, I must have been extremely heavy. I bet she thinks I'm someone else. The nerve of her! How dare she confuse me with someone else—am I not important enough to be remembered?' "

She realized that she had managed to mangle what would have been a compliment under any other circumstances. After the encounter she tried to step back and reflect on why she was reacting negatively. She realized that since early morning her self-perceptions were negative and these perceptions colored her ability to accept the other woman's comment at face value.

The story reflects a common experience and shows the effect that perceptions can have on feelings. Perceptions are filters through which we interpret reality. They are formed through our early life experiences and relationships, education and culture. The perceptions of the outer world are expressed as attitudes and prejudices and they affect how we relate with people. There are also perceptions of our inner world—the attitudes we hold about the person we "should" be. These filters can distort the way we see ourselves. It is the perceptions about self that can affect self-esteem negatively or positively. This can be seen in the above story. The speaker's view of herself does not allow her to hear the other person's words without bringing to them a negative connotation.

Looking back to the case study of the two sisters, the friend felt insecure about herself in her job. It was her perception of herself at that point that colored her ability to hear the other's suggestion as it was intended.

Feelings follow perceptions. In the following story we can see this statement borne out. On the first day of class, a teacher was lecturing to a classroom full of students. He was 15 minutes into the class when the door opened and another student entered the room. The teacher inwardly began to feel very angry. He perceived the student as rude and interpreted coming late to class as disrespectful behavior. He perceived the student's behavior as indicative of a belief that, as a teacher, he had nothing to offer the class. Through the remainder of the class, the teacher fed on his anger. At the end of class the student approached him and apologized for being late. As a new student unfamiliar with the campus, the student had mistakenly been sitting in the wrong class for the first ten minutes. As the teacher listened to the student's explanation, his anger dissipated. The teacher's perception of the situation triggered his feelings of anger toward the student. When he changed his perception, his emotion also changed.

As you reflect on your own personal experiences, are you aware of the degree to which your perceptions influence emotions? When you experience anger, do you take time to examine your inner self-perceptions that might be affecting your response, or do you place blame on the other?

Anger and Imagery

The role that imagery plays in anger is evident in the story of the two friends. As long as the sister allowed herself to dwell on the hurt she was experiencing, anger was her predominant and overwhelming emotion. Negative thoughts generate painful feelings. A person can choose to prolong angry feelings by recalling only negative experiences and feelings. These negative images only serve to fuel the anger of the moment.

The moment the sister changed her imagery and began to recall the beautiful memories of the relationship, her anger dissipated and was replaced by a desire for reconciliation. Positive thoughts generate pleasant feelings. A person who chooses to image beauty, calmness and joyful experiences will let go of the anger and, in turn, feel calm and joyful.

Emotions do not control a person. People have a powerful control over their emotional life. A person spontaneously experiences a certain emotion given particular stimuli. Through imagery and acts of the will, however, each person has a choice to continue to fuel that emotion or not. When one chooses to nurture negative images, the feelings perdure, thus creating a mood. In the case study, the sister made a deliberate choice to change the image she had of her friend. In doing so, she lessened the intensity of her anger and could look more objectively at the situation and its implications. Think about your last experience of feeling angry. What were the images that accompanied that feeling? Did you allow it to move into a mood?

Anger and Religiously Oriented People

The moral messages that each of us receives growing up become part of our self-evaluating internal mechanisms. The common difficulty with anger experienced by people from different cultures may well be exacerbated by the religious and moral overtones that are part of the educative process. The chapter on self-esteem will look at the dynamics that lead the religiously oriented person into difficulty with anger. This section will simply offer this belief for the reader's consideration. In your own experience do you find that a particular type of religious formation may have created a problem for your dealing with anger? What were the beliefs that were communicated and internalized? Do you still hold those beliefs?

It is interesting to note that the sister in the case study does not fall into our generalization about religiously oriented people. Quite the contrary, she does not pass judgment on her emotions nor does she censor them, but allows herself to experience a full range of emotions. She is not ashamed or adverse to exploring the scope of her emotions including anger, hatred and a desire to kill. Few would allow themselves to admit access of these emotions into consciousness. Fewer still would be free enough to share it with others. Having acknowledged her angry feelings, the sister could then enter into the process of dissipating that anger. Ultimately, she takes the initiative to approach her friend in a nondefensive way to seek reconciliation. These mature behaviors can serve as a model for what is possible for all of us.

We attended a block association meeting in a large, multi-ethnic neighborhood. During the meeting the neighbors were quite honest, open and direct in venting their anger toward those present whom they believed deserved it. The meetings were traditionally spiced with frequent and intense conflicts. As soon as the meeting ended, the participants would gather socially. Seemingly, however, there was no residue from the expressions of anger and hostility that dotted the meeting. We left the meeting with the fantasy of inviting those participants to conduct sessions for communities, pastoral councils and parish staffs. We envisioned their assisting these religious groups to deal with anger and conflict in ways that did not dominate the social aspect of their relationships or interfere with their ability to carry out the Lord's work more collaboratively.

Anger and Regression

When the sister in the case study we looked at earlier described herself as acting "like a four year old," several others at the workshop resonated with her feeling. A number of them recalled similar incidents of anger in their own lives. They, too, described their reactions to anger as juvenile. Initially, the realization and revelations were accompanied by ripples of anxious laughter. When the leaders pointed out that the laughter might be coming from feelings of embarrassment, the participants were reluctant to agree. They became defensive and, believing that it is inappropriate and immature for adults to react as children, denied behaving this way. In the discussion that followed, the group members disengaged themselves from the defensive stance that protected them from admitting to childish behavior. They saw that when anger is experienced the initial reaction is to revert to the attitudes, emotions and behaviors appropriate to an early period of development.

Consider times in your own life when you have felt most angry. What did you feel and how did you behave? Anger is an extremely primitive emotion. It is one of the first emotions experienced. When a baby's need for food, warmth or freedom from discomfort is frustrated or not instantly gratified, the baby expresses anger. Consider the intensity of emotional response from a two year old when a parent refuses to accede to the child's demands. Remnants of that primitive emotion remain into adulthood and resurface when we experience frustration or other anger-producing experiences. In a way each new experience of anger hurdles us through a time warp into a frame of mind, emotion and response that resides in our long-suppressed or repressed unconscious.

Difficulties occur because emotions are immediately acted upon without sufficient reflection. Any emotion that does not receive adequate attention or reflection leads to behavior that is usually regressive and destructive to growth within ourselves or relationships.

It should not come as a surprise when we find ourselves behaving as we did at an earlier age. Rather, it should warn us that our reaction indicates the presence of an extremely well-defended, anxiety-producing primitive emotion.

We recently heard the story of a young businessman in group therapy. During the course of the therapy it became obvious that his abnormal and paralyzing fear of anger was one of the major detriments to a fuller, more productive life. Continued probing to discover the reason for such an incapacitating fear of anger initially bore little insight. After many months, the client realized that whenever anger was discussed in the group, he experienced a strong and, at times, even physical reaction. He began to perspire, his body became stiff, his palms became moist and his heart began to pound rapidly. He was anxious. Observing how other members of the group explored their experiences of anger, he finally unearthed a long-suppressed childhood desire to kill his younger brother.

He recalled one day when he saw his brother receive attention previously reserved exclusively for him. He experienced a strong urge to throw his brother into the swimming pool and let him drown. He did not act on the feeling, of course, but when he realized that he could have such a violent feeling, an overpowering fear and anxiety resulted. His feeling of wanting to kill his brother would have lost him the love and affection of his parents. The fear of the repercussions caused him to quickly bury the desire in the recesses of his unconscious. It was buried but not forgotten. It resurfaced as a dependable, unfailing, but emotionally counterproductive deterrent that prevented him from ever permitting himself to acknowledge anger. Unconsciously, he maintained an erroneous fear and belief that if he ever allowed himself to experience anger, he might hurt or kill someone.

Although this example may be an extreme one, it offers an important lesson. Anger can often produce extremely primitive thinking and behavior. One should not be surprised, nor should one condemn oneself for responding in such primitive ways. Hopefully, one can use the opportunity for reflection and subsequent growth. When you become angry, how do you react? How would an objective observer describe your reactions and behaviors? Is it the mature reaction of an adult? Can you accept the infantile aspect of the reaction without any need to defend or judge? Are you willing to examine the genesis of the reaction?

Anger as a Precondition for Conflict

In the epistle of St. James (4:1-4) the writer offers a rhetorical question, "Where do all these wars and battles between yourselves first start?" He provides an answer and tells the recipients of this letter that it starts within themselves. He suggests that they want things, and since they cannot always obtain them, they kill one another. St. James was a wise observer of human nature. He realized that most quarrels, fights and conflicts are a direct result of acting on anger. He also hypothesized that it was the anger resulting from this frustration that resulted in the violent behavior he witnessed in some of the local Christian communities.

What St. James observes is the predictable chain reaction of frustration producing anger, the anger being converted into hostility, the hostility directed toward those to whom we feel angry. The recipient of the hostility begins the process all over, leading to an intensification of the emotion and response in the initiating party, and ending in conflict.

Think of times when you have found yourself in conflict. Ask yourself what you were experiencing and feeling at that time. Almost all conflict is immediately preceded by feelings of anger on the part of all participants. Returning again to our case study, it is evident that both sisters were feeling hurt and anger, and this is what precipitated the conflict. If a person does not feel angry, he or she usually cannot be provoked into a fight. However, the normal dynamic is that the person who initially feels angry attacks the other. This produces a feeling of anger in the other. Then both parties, in a stance of protecting themselves and wanting to hurt the other, lash out. Conflict results.

Anger does not always produce conflict. There are other options. The two sisters, for example, could have behaved in an even more immature way. They could have reverted to punishment through hostile silence. This type of response is sometimes expressed in families and among people in ministry. Rather than deal directly with conflict that could lead to dialogue and ultimately growth for both parties, a wall of silence is erected between the two. Another response could have been to withdraw before hostilely expressing their hurt, but arranging to come together again and dialogue at a time when they were feeling more in control of their emotional response. They eventually did come together to talk. Perhaps it would have been even more productive if they had not initially vented their emotions.

Think of a recent conflict in which you were engaged. What were you feeling before the conflict? Anger? How else could you have responded? If you were to experience the same situation today, what would you do differently?

Anger as Related to Human Needs

The key to understanding human behavior is in the area of human needs. Remembering that most behavior is directed toward achieving some basic need can help to make sense out of what appear as inane or senseless acts. In the case under scrutiny, it is not difficult to track the needs involved. The sister reporting the story felt her self-esteem threatened when her friend shouted at her and criticized her. She perceived this as a put-down. Her desire to avenge and hurt the other was also an attempt, at best feeble, to bolster her sagging self-esteem. Her desire for reconciliation came from a variety of psycho-social needs for love, belonging and intimacy. Her friend was also functioning from a need-protecting stance. Inasmuch as we do not know her perception of the incident, we can only hypothesize what dynamics were operative. It would seem that she perceived her friend's suggestions as an attack on her own competency. Her outburst would probably represent a desire to protect her needs for security and self-esteem.

We have followed the anger of the two sisters in the case study to model a method that can enable readers to explore their own needs that are threatened when anger is experienced. This model can lead to a greater understanding of and insight into anger in life. As we pointed out above, anger frequently results in conflict and is generally related to one specific need: the need for self-esteem. Think of a time you were engaged in conflict. What was the need involved? Were you aware of that need as the core of the conflict? How would you deal now with the conflict?

Anger and Conflict Can Be Handled Effectively

The two sisters in the scenario are not unique in the manner in which they handled their anger and the conflict that followed. We have had the opportunity to work with many groups in conflict. In all these cases the groups have been able to address and in most cases to manage the conflict. Working through conflict is never an easy task, for conflict is usually frightening and messy.

One major condition required for individuals and groups to work through conflict is to establish a climate of safety and security. Safety and security are among the most primitive human needs. People will not risk exploring the antecedents of their anger or the behavior that results from anger until they trust that these basic needs are not threatened. Often it is only in the secure and safe environment of an intimate friendship, spiritual direction, counseling or therapy that people will feel free enough to explore the meaning of their anger. Looking again to our case study, it was because the women shared a deep friendship that they were able to risk not only expressing their anger but, more importantly, initiating reconciliation.

Handling one's own anger constructively is but one part of the equation. Dealing with anger that is directed toward me or assisting a person struggling with anger can be as difficult as grappling with one's own emotion. When faced with the anger of another, the challenge is to avoid two instinctive reactions. The first inclination is to react to the person's behavior. This is counterproductive because it puts both people in a defensive posture. The presence of anger indicates that the person has experienced hurt in some form. Attempting to look beyond a person's behavior to the reason for the hurt is more productive.

The second instinctive reaction is to label the person as an angry person. Anger is a painful emotion: It hurts. When one can respond compassionately to the pain experienced by another, anger is defused. Generally, a compassionate response creates a climate where a person is willing to dialogue and talk about the pain and hurt. Because of moralistic or negative connotations of anger, labeling someone as an angry person only increases the hurt and fortifies the defensive posture.

Relationship Between Anger and Growth

Because of the two sisters' desire to heal a relationship that had been broken by anger and conflict they arrived at a "sacramental moment"—a unique experience when there is a simultaneous encounter of God and the other person. Anger and conflict do not always have to be divisive. Anger and conflict can spark greater self-knowledge and an appreciation of others in my life. When these moments are reflected upon and discussed, as they were in the case study, they can draw those involved into a deeper relationship. What transpires between individuals after anger and conflict have erupted depends primarily on the beliefs and attitudes of those involved. When the belief is that anger and conflict are inevitably destructive and innately evil, probably no growth will occur. The search for the presence of God in anger and conflict can lead one ultimately to discover new life.

It is the pain that comes from anger and conflict that causes us to resist the exploration that leads to new growth. Avoidance is a normal reaction. Yet by avoiding what we think will produce pain, we may be running away from the discovery of a source of gift and grace.

In a talk several years ago, Sister Theresa Kane suggested that "The core of courage is rage. . . . For each of us I pray for a passionate, holy rage; a just anger in the face of injustice, not confused with hatred and hostility." Sister Kane identifies the crux of the matter. Anger and rage can be a gift of God, one that is potentially life-giving and energizing for action. Sister Kane states the obvious, but often elusive, differentiation between anger and hostility. The two are not synonymous. Feeling angry does not imply that the anger must be automatically converted into hostility or hatred. Hostility is always a choice, but it is not the only choice. When anger is experienced, the option to express anger constructively is always present. Recall a time in your life when anger led to growth. Why was this so? What can I learn for future situations?

Forgiveness

The case study came to a happy conclusion because the sister's goal was to seek forgiveness and reconciliation. The ultimate goal for all Christians is forgiveness—to seek reconciliation not only with oneself and with God, but with the people in our daily life. This issue is of such importance that we will devote the next chapter to the subject.

Summary

While anger is a normal emotion, it is complex, unpleasant, frequently painful and often messy. Therefore, the immediate reaction of many individuals to this feeling is to deny or avoid it. Hopefully, as a result of demythologizing anger you are more convinced of its capacity to be life-giving. When a person is courageous and deals with anger it can become a source of life. The willingness to deal with anger begins with the beliefs that anger can be life-giving and that one has the capacity to deal effectively and constructively with it. When people allow the messy aspects of the emotion to deter them from entering into anger, life will stagnate.

Reflection Questions

What are my beliefs about anger?

Do I allow myself to experience intense feelings of anger, or do I push them down and pretend they don't exist?

When I feel angry do I check out my own perceptions of the situation?

Can I identify a time when anger and conflict have led me to self-awareness and growth?

Chapter Three

Forgiveness: New Life

A distinguishing mark of Christians should be the presence of forgiveness and the willingness to seek reconciliation, not the absence of anger and conflict in their lives. The concept of *willingness* to seek reconciliation cannot be overlooked, for in some situations reconciliation will not be possible. Reconciliation is a two-way process into which I cannot force another. I can forgive, but I cannot demand that the other forgive me in return. Webster's *New Collegiate Dictionary* defines forgiveness as "a process of ceasing to feel resentment against someone or to pardon someone."

The choice to let go of resentment is to choose life. It is holding on to anger and resentment that ultimately dulls the life within us. The choice to forgive brings with it a feeling of relief, a freedom of spirit and renewed life. It is often the one who forgives rather than the person who is forgiven who receives the greater benefit.

Anger, hostility and conflict are all part of the human condition. It is unrealistic to think that anyone will reach a point in this mortal life when these elements will be completely absent. In one report of the Notre Dame study on the parish we read a rather startling statement: "The absence of conflict in some parishes (and by extension any Christian group) is more likely a sign of *rigor mortis* than of vitality and community."[1] Contrary to popular belief, the presence of anger or conflict is not automatically emotionally draining. These two feared dynamics are not indicators of death, but signs of the presence of life. It is the absence of forgiveness that condemns one to a lifeless existence.

The previous chapters looked at the various alternatives for handling anger. Feelings of anger can be stored away or they can be discharged either constructively or destructively. One way of constructively expressing feelings of anger is through forgiveness. Forgiveness has been the topic of study among anthropologists and religious writers for centuries, but until recently there has been little reference in psychological literature to the relationship between anger and forgiveness. This attitude may stem from a bias on the part of some psychologically oriented professionals that religious insights are not relevant in the mental health field. Richard P. Fitzgibbons, in an article entitled "The Cognitive and Emotive Uses of Forgiveness in the Treatment of Anger,"[2] suggests that the most effective way of dealing with anger is to help people learn to forgive. The normal reaction to frustration, abuse, threat and injustice is the desire to get even and hurt the person whom we believe has caused the pain and hurt. Forgiveness is a learned, not a natural, response. More accurately, it is a supernatural response.

We are deeply indebted to Dr. Fitzgibbons for providing such profound insights regarding forgiveness. Much of the material that will be developed in this chapter has been influenced by his writing.

The Magic and Misconceptions of Forgiveness

For the Christian, the most life-giving expression of anger is forgiveness. The process of forgiveness is more difficult and complex than some religious writers and spiritual directors might convey. In some religious literature forgiveness is presented as an almost magical solution to many of the human and spiritual problems that afflict human beings. The literature presents forgiveness as achieved through a simple act of the will that causes little problem or anxiety. In reality, forgiveness involves all a person's faculties: the mind, the emotions, the memory and, finally, the will.

Over the centuries many misconceptions have developed around the process of forgiveness. We can begin this discussion by reviewing some misconceptions and reflect upon the effect they may have on one's ability to forgive.

The first misconception is that anger will be forever dissipated at the moment one forgives. The process of healing and forgetting is extremely slow and usually lasts longer than would be expected. Long after one has forgiven self and others, traces of the emotion of anger remain. You may forgive someone for a hurt, for example, and at a later time, when thinking about the situation that caused the hurt, find yourself again experiencing anger. The mind can accept the slow process of dissipation of anger long before the heart is comfortable with this reality.

Another misconception is that the act of forgiveness lifts a burden from the other person. The opposite is true. The person offering forgiveness most strongly experiences a sense of relief. Perhaps you have had the experience of approaching someone to say that you have forgiven him or her. You assume that the other would be overjoyed, thankful and relieved to learn of your "compassionate" decision. You experience a shock when you realize that the person not only was unaware of the angry feelings but, even worse, didn't even remember the incident that you claim caused your anger.

The decision to forgive is an act of compassion toward oneself. If anger is not released, it perdures and causes the spiritual, emotional and physical damage to self which was discussed earlier. Forgiveness of self in some ways may be the most difficult aspect of forgiveness. Many people set standards of excellence for themselves that are unrealistic and unattainable. This can lead one to be overly demanding and unforgiving of self. This is especially true for people in ministry who are unwilling to forgive themselves for any moral lapses. Ministers are the most compassionate human beings when dealing with others' pain and hurt. Compassion toward themselves, however, is often sadly absent.

People who cannot be compassionate toward themselves and who extract unreasonable demands on mind, body and soul ultimately destroy themselves. One of the most glaring examples screamed out from the headline of a sports page: "Runner Attempts Suicide." The story described a woman who held a national collegiate record for long-distance running. The article told of her destructive behavior when she could not live up to her personal goals and expectations. In the middle of a race, she suddenly left the track, jogged across the infield onto a nearby bridge, and eventually leapt from the bridge, suffering a serious spinal cord injury. The author of the article speculated that because she was a perfectionist and did not feel as though she was doing her best in the race, she became despondent and decided to end her life. Fortunately, this extreme behavior is rare. Yet, many engage in less fatal though self-destructive behavior because the unrealistic and inflated ideals remain beyond their reach.

A final misconception is that forgiveness is complete only when there is communication with another. Forgiveness is primarily an act of the will and an inner decision to divest oneself of self-destructive emotions. The primary action of forgiveness is a personal decision. This decision begins a process of divesting oneself of the desire for revenge and retribution. When this desire for revenge has produced alienation in significant relationships, seeking and expressing forgiveness can help to overcome the alienation and renew the relationship. The actual verbalization of forgiveness is not essential, since forgiveness is an inner transformation.

Therapeutic Aspects of Forgiveness

Forgiveness has a twofold therapeutic effect. On the one hand, it frees a person from painful emotions and destructive impulses; on the other, it helps one to be more creative and life-giving in relationships.

First, forgiveness can free one from painful memories. We recently met a priest from Yugoslavia who related his experience of this dynamic. The year he was ordained the Communists occupied his hometown and murdered his mother, father and seven brothers and sisters. He admitted that it took five years before he decided to forgive the man who was responsible for murdering his family. It was almost 25 years before he returned to Yugoslavia for a visit and searched for the man who had killed his family. Upon encountering this man, the priest threw his arms around him and told him that he had forgiven him. As he recounted the story, tears appeared in the eyes of his listeners, tears that probably conveyed myriad emotions and realizations. There was awe at the radical aspect of forgiveness that the priest possessed. This priest was free from the animosity and desire for revenge that might be expected in one who had experienced such excruciating pain. There was a sense of shame and sadness in those of us who still found it difficult to forgive people in our lives for insignificant reasons. Coupled with this was the challenge to grow to be more the forgiving people God has called each of us to be, emulating Jesus' own ultimate forgiveness from the cross, "Father, forgive them, for they know not what they do." This priest, through his peace and joy, was a living model of the therapeutic effects of forgiveness.

Memories of pain, hurt and injury can undermine a person's freedom and can become the controlling force in life. Recall, if you will, coming into the presence of a person toward whom you harbor deep feelings of anger and resentment. Unconsciously, you may discover your thoughts obsessed with that person. As the memories flash across the mind's screen, the emotions, pain and hurt of the past are resurrected and re-experienced in the present. If not dealt with, these emotions, memories and thoughts can become obsessive to the point where they control actions. At these times a person can behave in ways that are uncharacteristic and damaging to self-esteem.

Of all the emotions, anger has a pervasive quality that can seize a person's life and affect interactions. For example, a pastor can have an exceptionally difficult pastoral council meeting that leaves him feeling angry. He might displace those angry feelings and find himself snapping at his secretary, or staff, or any unfortunate parishioner who might innocently wander onto the scene. The intensity of anger can result in acting out with more force and violence than the situation warrants, or than he intends. The decision to forgive can free him of the misdirected and misplaced anger that only inflames his feelings of self-deprecation.

In addition, anger stimulates and produces two other painful and uncomfortable emotions: guilt and anxiety. Guilt, as will be seen in the chapter on self-esteem, is often the result of failing to live up to an ego ideal, that is, one the idealized self has. The experience of guilt is extremely painful. Religiously oriented people often feel guilty for even feeling angry. This feeling is compounded when one also experiences a feeling of resentment, a desire for revenge and an unwillingness to forgive. When a choice of forgiveness is made, angry feelings gradually begin to dissipate, and guilt feelings diminish. Religiously oriented people who have learned the preeminent place of forgiveness in their religion will, of course, feel even more guilty when they resist forgiveness.

Anxiety as discussed in the previous chapter is not only a painful emotion but a confusing one. Anxiety is that fear-like emotion that occurs whenever we begin to think about doing something contrary to the ego ideal, the idealized self. The problem with anxiety is that the source of the emotion is never conscious, and therefore is often more perplexing and confusing than other emotions. When anger triggers anxiety, the result is a web of emotions such as anger, resentment and revenge. The internal monitoring mechanism immediately sends the message that a good Christian shouldn't feel these things. The person's defense system is activated; the "unwanted" emotions are stifled; anxiety then becomes the predominant feeling.

Forgiveness creates a sense of freedom and vitality which is conducive to building up the positive aspects of life. Primarily, it frees one to build relationships. The longer one retains anger, the more it interferes with the ability to enter into loving, positive, constructive relationships.

Reasons for Holding Onto Anger and Not Forgiving

Why would any mature person choose to hold onto anger and resist forgiveness? Surprisingly, there are a number of secondary gains for someone to hold onto anger. The term "secondary gain" describes a dynamic where the behavior of a person seems, to all appearances, nonproductive or counterproductive. However, in a strange way it benefits the person involved.

One benefit is that anger protects a person from more painful or more fearful emotions. For some, sadness and loneliness are more difficult emotions to admit and deal with than is anger. As long as anger is the dominant emotion, a person can avoid looking at other emotions such as sadness, loneliness and emptiness that may be present. An unconscious logic dictates that it is better to be angry than to be sad or lonely.

Anger can also be a cover and safeguard for other phenomena and dynamics. Maintaining anger can, for instance, protect one from facing some underlying inadequacy. Perhaps you have encountered individuals who seem to be perpetually angry and are quick to share that anger. The more they focus on and retain their anger, the less they have to face the painful reality of their own inadequacies. Yet, in their presence one often feels there is more sadness than anger. It is apparent to everyone but themselves that the anger is merely a cover-up for their feelings of inadequacy. For these people forgiveness is unacceptable. Forgiveness would take away their defense and force them to deal with the ego-threatening reality of their inadequacy as they perceive it.

Perhaps the greatest value of not forgiving for some people in ministry is that it protects them from having to face the deadly reality of sadness and depression. Unfortunately, a great many people suffer from depression, albeit at times a very low-grade depression. A psychiatrist who treats many people in ministry stated that almost without exception his patients who were professional ministers suffered from depression. This certainly does not mean that all ministers are depressed, but rather where there is a tendency toward mental illness, depression will probably be the most frequent diagnosis. Depression can run an entire continuum from feeling a little sad to a psychotic depression, which can fully incapacitate a person. A low-grade depression is one that is characterized by a mood of sadness, general fatigue and listlessness, lack of excitement, and, often, eating and sleeping disorders. Depression is one of the most painful experiences a person can endure. If you have ever talked with a person suffering from depression, you are aware of the absolute and profound effect it has on its victim. The description offered is one of complete hopelessness and, at times, helplessness. This is a state so painful that even anger is preferable. People who have an awareness of their underlying depression hold onto their anger and resist forgiveness, which would force them to deal with this painful reality. As we indicated earlier, anger is energy. Depressed people who are aware that they are lifeless and barely existing will choose anger, for it provides them with energy and assures them that they are still alive.

Another benefit for holding on to anger is that it keeps others at a distance. There are many people in ministry and in community who fear intimacy. One of the most successful defenses against intimacy is anger. No one wants to get close to someone who is always angry and frequently hostile. Some of the cynical, angry people encountered in community and ministry have unconsciously developed this defense as a way of keeping themselves from facing the more fearful reality of intimacy.

Anger provides some other interesting secondary gains. Anger often gains attention, controls others in the sphere of our influence, and provides the opportunity to wallow in self-pity.

People who have an intense hunger for attention and who feel neglected and unimportant would do anything to capture attention. Their behavior is not unlike that of a little child demanding parental attention. These people have frequently discovered that to the extent they maintain and express their anger, they will hold center stage, thus convincing themselves of their own importance. This need for attention and control can be expressed in a variety of ways: tirades, temper tantrums, shouting, pouting, silence, sulking, withdrawal, petulance, combativeness and competitiveness.

Worse still, this infantile angry behavior will often control people in ways that could not be otherwise achieved. Power over others gives the person a feeling of strength. There is a sad irony in this. Because this infantile behavior gains the immediate attention and control the person desires, he or she assumes this behavior as a normal pattern of functioning. In the long run, however, this provokes anger and hostility in others. Some community or ministry members who fear anger and hostility allow themselves to be dominated and controlled rather than challenging and confronting. This reinforces the dysfunctional behavior. Others may choose to distance themselves or to ignore or neglect the person displaying inappropriate behavior. These actions only serve to increase the angry feelings and underline the person's belief of being unimportant and neglected.

Indulgence in self-pity can also be a secondary gain for people who choose to hold on to their anger. Self-pity is narcissistic, while forgiveness demands looking beyond self and becoming involved in the lives of others. Christian charity is alive when caring enough about each other results in confronting the behavior that is self-destructive.

Regardless of the reason chosen for holding onto anger, it is important to remember that such a decision is self-destructive. A talk show host recently railed against a suggestion from Bishop Tutu, the South African Nobel Prize winner, when Bishop Tutu suggested that Jews forgive Hitler for the atrocities he inflicted on their people. Aware of the value that Jews place on the need to remember, Bishop Tutu was asking them to forgive, not necessarily forget what had happened. The talk show host, outraged by the suggestion, began to facetiously suggest that other victims of oppression should also forgive their long-dead oppressors. He failed to understand Bishop Tutu's point that forgiveness does not affect those being forgiven as much as those doing the forgiving. A failure to forgive, like other intense emotions, can have serious physiological consequences.

The Process of Forgiveness

The realization of the beneficial aspects of forgiveness and the actual decision to forgive another embarks a person on a process involving the three faculties of cognition, emotion and will. The process moves from the person being convinced of the need to forgive, to becoming involved in the life of another, to bringing some resolution to the pain of anger.

The initial step is cognitive. There can be numerous benefits for the one who forgives. The realization of these benefits—emotional health, inner peace, spiritual growth, the healing of a fragmented relationship—can lead to an intellectual assent. The internalization of the belief in forgiveness can lead to the desire to claim that value as a force in one's life. From intellectual involvement, a person moves outside self to involvement with others.

The second step is the conscious decision to understand the person whom one desires to forgive. Understanding can be one of the most therapeutic aspects of the entire process. Attempting to see a situation from another's point of view can change the original emotion as well as a person's perspective. Stepping into another's shoes, so to speak, can help to understand the feelings of the other person that motivated the hurtful actions. Trying to understand another can lead to empathy and result in freedom from the existing anger.

Using the intellect to attempt to understand another, whether or not that is ever verbalized, begins the cognitive process of forgiveness.

As a person becomes intellectually involved in understanding another, the emotions quickly come into play. There may be an initial desire to avoid forgiveness. The more intense the emotion, the stronger the ambivalence. An intellectual assent to go forward toward forgiveness is coupled with an automatic response to run away from, avoid or deny any painful emotion.

At this point the faculty of the will is involved. The capacity to choose is one of the greatest God-given gifts human beings possess. This third step of resolution is the point of decision: whether to hold on to the anger or to forgive. Either choice has its implications. There may be a choice not to forgive. This need not be out of malice but can be for other reasons such as important secondary gains, lack of personal freedom and fear. In either case this choice leaves a person unhealed. The anger will be resurrected each time the person remembers the situation, the hurt or the person who caused it.

The choice to forgive, whether or not that forgiveness is expressed to another, brings with it a sense of relief and a feeling of a burden lifted. This relief is short-lived, however, and followed quickly by a barrage of other emotions. Surprisingly, sadness may be the strongest emotion to surface at this point. There is a real sense of loss in letting go of the desire for revenge. This can be followed by a strong sense of guilt, arising from an assumption that if forgiveness had really occurred, all desire for revenge would be gone. Forgiveness is not, as we said earlier, an instantaneous, magical process. The movement from anger to a less intense emotion is a very slow one.

Obstacles to Forgiveness

Even when there is a conscious decision to attempt forgiveness, one will probably find a variety of resistances and obstacles. Some of these will be internal and some external.

It is impossible to forgive unless one has first accepted the fact that one has felt anger over being wronged. One of the major internal obstacles to forgiveness is the unwillingness to admit the emotion of anger. The study undertaken by the bishops of the United States on the priests in this country[3] indicated that the greatest problem of the priests was not being in touch with and accepting their feelings and needs, especially their aggressive impulses. In other words, priests—and, based on our experience in the United States and other countries, we would add, most ministers—find it difficult to admit anger.

A few years ago one of the authors conducted a retreat for resigned priests and their wives. In the course of the weekend the wives met together. They discovered a common difficulty: These men still had trouble dealing with anger. This was true for those who had recently left the active priestly ministry, as well as those who had been married for a number of years. As we pointed out in the previous chapter, most religiously oriented people have trouble admitting that they feel this very human emotion. Unless a person can admit and accept the feeling of anger at the hurt one has experienced, forgiveness is impossible.

Some of the myths about anger influence not only the ability to admit the emotion, but also the freedom to forgive. When people are asked to imagine anger, they usually describe it with extreme, violent fantasies. They find it difficult to conceive of anger as anything but extreme and violent. It is the fear of this intensity that often blocks the process of forgiveness.

Another obstacle to achieving forgiveness and reconciliation is the inability to admit being the one who erred and needs to be forgiven for causing hurt to another. Because so much of the self-esteem of ministers is tied up with their ministry, it becomes difficult to admit errors in ministry. If one is unable to admit to having done anything wrong, there is no need for forgiveness.

Obstacles to forgiveness do not reside only within the self. There are also external obstacles. A major obstacle is the lack of models, especially parental ones. For one who has never witnessed parents being able to forgive, the concept of forgiving others is illusive. In the parable of the prodigal son our Christian faith teaches the idea of a forgiving God, but the lived reality of many people may lack concrete models. Add to that the lack of models in churches and communities, and the problem is compounded.

We had the opportunity to witness a model of forgiveness. At the conclusion of a gathering for clergy, the bishop of the diocese announced an unfinished task. He acknowledged that in his role as bishop he had unknowingly and unwillingly hurt some of those present. He declared he would search out the men he had hurt and beg their forgiveness. With a twinkle in his eye, he then announced that as the bishop he knew there wasn't a man in the room who had not hurt someone else in that room. He challenged them to follow his example and search out someone they had hurt and ask forgiveness. It was a powerful sight: one hundred eighty priests, some in tears, going to each other to ask forgiveness! The model of forgiveness their leader showed them enabled those priests to ask forgiveness of each other. Moreover, the bishop went one step further: He asked their forgiveness. To forgive another is, in some way, relatively easy, for it implies that the other was wrong, and I was right. To seek forgiveness from another is an indication that I was wrong and this is a sign of maturity.

The expectations that a person places upon others can be an obstacle to forgiveness. There may be the expectation that the other who has caused hurt will change his or her manner, behavior or opinion. It is extremely difficult to forgive when there is no indication of change in the other. There are usually only three possible options:

—to change the situation,

—to change the other,

—to change self.

Most people do not have sufficient control over situations to change them substantially or dramatically. Whenever the goal is to change the other person, frustration and more anger is certain. This is especially true if the other is a well-disciplined passive-aggressive person. Realistically, the only thing over which anyone has control is oneself. Often in forgiving another there is a conscious or unconscious expectation that the other will change. When change does not happen, it fuels anger and resentment, making the process of forgiveness that much more difficult.

Indications of Progress

A freedom from and lessening of the intensity of the painful emotion of anger is a measure of progress in the spirit of forgiveness. This can be seen concretely in several ways.

One of the first indicators of growth is the ability to express anger appropriately. Too often one's personalized expectations of the expression of anger are unrealistic or excessive. What appears to the one expressing the anger as overly intense and inappropriate may appear to others as mild and appropriate.

The ability to approach others more easily or readily to ask forgiveness is another sign of progress. Sometimes one's fantasies about how others will respond if one asks forgiveness impedes the willingness to take this initiative. When those fantasies are not realized, it is more likely that one will overcome the initial resistance to asking forgiveness and seeking reconciliation. Progress is being made when there is a shorter interim between hurtful behavior and a willingness to risk making oneself vulnerable in asking for forgiveness.

A third indication of progress is revealed when a person no longer feels controlled by anger nor is fearful of its expression. Fear of anger and its expression absorb a great deal of the energy that could be more appropriately and creatively given to family, ministry and community. A common complaint heard from lay and religious in ministry is their tiredness and lack of energy. When there is a diminishment in fear, there is often a corresponding increase in energy.

Another indication of progress is the lessening of pain and anxiety as compared with previous experience. This also brings a sense of greater freedom. Anger with its accompanying pain no longer dominates one's life in the way it once did. We heard the story recently of a discerning and perceptive spiritual director who had been meeting with a directee over the course of a year. Having listened to the repetition of the directee's all-consuming description of pain and anxiety, the director simply declared, "You are more than your pain." The directee realized that he had become obsessed with the pain to the point of missing many of the beautiful experiences in his own life.

The ability to move more easily into loving relationships is another indication of progress. For some celibate ministers this will never be easy. There has to be a conviction that one of the primary needs of every human person is to love and be loved. Pope John Paul II has declared, "Man cannot live without love. He remains a being that is incomprehensible for himself, his life is senseless, if love is not revealed to him, if he does not encounter love, if he does not experience it, if he does not participate intimately in it." [4]

In addition there has to be commitment to the philosophy that one can become a compassionate and other-centered minister only to the extent that one is able to enter into loving relations. For those ministers who have used their anger as a protection against intimacy, this is a fearful step. "To love another person is to see the face of God," proclaims Jean Valjean in *Les Miserables.* The scene has a profound impact, but it is more than a clever theatrical moment: It is reality! Only when we learn to truly love, perhaps, can we truly forgive, and only when we learn to forgive are we truly free to love.

In the course of learning forgiveness a strange reaction can occur. Although the forgiveness is taking place in the present, there is an aura of the past that seems to pervade the situation. Often in the process, one is confronted with the reality that one is not only forgiving this particular person in the present, but there are memories and images of persons and situations from the past that float into consciousness and become part of the present. This is a normal experience and a sign of real progress. This reaction stems from childhood, when defense mechanisms were used to deny some of the intense feelings of anger directed toward primary care-givers, those people upon whom we were so dependent for our very life. Often in the process of forgiving, a person is confronted with an awareness of past hurts. It is a positive sign if one can first admit the presence of these past hurts and then be willing to forgive those toward whom there is past anger. Anger that is repressed remains as unfinished business. Admitting past hurts, however, is especially difficult when the forgiveness involves parents or parent surrogates who have been idealized. There may even be feelings of guilt in admitting that these idealized figures have caused hurt. The more intense the reaction and anger, the more likely that the anger is only partially directed to the person in the present. In all likelihood, it is directed unconsciously toward those significant people from the past. Unless unfinished business from the past is acknowledged, it will probably be difficult, if not impossible, to develop an attitude of forgiveness.

Growth is also evident in recognizing that simply expressing anger does not necessarily dissipate the feeling. There are people who express their anger ad nauseam, perhaps hoping that eventually there will be a catharsis and release of the anger. Expressing anger does not change the internal self-destructive dynamics. There must be a decision to do something different, to forgive.

The final indication of progress is experiencing pity, empathy or compassion for the other. The psyche cannot maintain two conflicting emotions at the same time, so a person cannot feel anger and at the same time experience pity, empathy or compassion. To pity others is to feel sorry for them. To empathize is to feel what they feel. Compassion is more than a feeling, however; it is a spiritual response in which we attempt to do something to assuage that pain because we feel for the other's pain. Feeling pity or empathy or expressing compassion is the beginning of the process of forgiveness.

We witnessed an example of this when we had the opportunity and privilege of conducting a program with an outstanding cleric who had been subjected to intense criticism, judgment and condemnation. Others discussed his predicament, usually raining their anger, hostility and resentment on the church officials who had abused and treated him in an un-Christian and unjust way. The seeming defenders communicated no sense of forgiveness for either church officials or the institutional church. Rather, they seethed with anger and hostility, bereft of any compassion or forgiveness. While they demanded compassion for this man, they were uncompassionate. They appeared as avenging angels, ready to destroy all those who had been unjust. The unjustly treated cleric, on the other hand, displayed none of the intense emotions toward those who had abused him. What was most evident was the man's deep spirituality, peace and universal empathy and compassion. Obviously he had reached the stage of forgiveness, and thus felt a sense of freedom and life.

Forgiveness in the Christian Community

The psychologist Abraham Maslow claims that if people are going to grow they need two things: models and challenge.[5] There is no question that people in leadership in the Christian community are quick to challenge others to grow, but do we as leaders provide the necessary models for forgiveness? It is our conviction that Christian communities do not fulfill their purpose for existence in the church if their members are not given to reconciliation. They have a responsibility to witness to universal reconciliation for the church.

Leaders have a serious responsibility to witness to the other members of the Christian community what it means to be a forgiving person. There is an example of this in the missionary sister who was working with peasants who were being oppressed and murdered. As a result of a junta, the oppressors were ousted and many of them landed in jail. While the normal reaction of the families of those who had been beaten and murdered was revenge, a different scenario resulted. The sister organized these families to minister to their former oppressors now in jail. She witnessed what it means to be a forgiving person, and through her witness was able to assist these families to grow also in Christian forgiveness.

To become a forgiving person demands a high level of maturity. One of us had recently presented a workshop on anger and forgiveness, only to return home to the community and become engaged in a painful, immature, angry outburst with another member:

> In the process I managed to do everything opposite from what I had instructed others. After a short cooling off period, the other person came to me and requested that we meet in a couple of days, after we both had time to reflect. He was mature enough to initiate a process of reconciliation in spite of the inherent risks. He began the dialogue by admitting his own culpability and asking for forgiveness. After we had become reconciled, he promised that this would never happen again. I then promised him that it would!

Human beings have emotions and will become angry and hurt one another. This is part of what it means to be human. It is okay to become angry. The question is, can we forgive?

While Dr. Fitzgibbons suggests that forgiveness makes sense from a psychological perspective, Christians have an even greater reason to forgive. The challenge and models for forgiveness are found in the scriptures. Forgiveness is of the very essence of scripture and, therefore, what we are about as Christians. The culmination of the scriptural lesson on forgiveness occurs when the crucified, dying Jesus, as part of his final prayer, says, "Father, forgive them for they know not what they do." This brings to completion what he challenged us to do in prayer: Be radical enough when praying to God in heaven to ask to be forgiven only to the degree that we forgive others. When we fully appreciate what we are asking for, it should produce fear within us. Throughout his public life and ministry, Jesus witnessed to what it means to be a forgiving person. He unremittingly forgave the woman taken in adultery, he counseled Peter to be far more forgiving than Peter would ever have considered, to forgive seven times seventy times—a metaphor for infinite forgiveness. No matter how often we are hurt, our challenge as Christians is always to forgive. Jesus not only modeled what it meant to be a forgiving person, he continually taught, especially through parables, the necessity of forgiveness.

One of the best known of all the parables is the story of the prodigal son or, more aptly, the forgiving father, whose forgiveness was unlimited. In the parable of the unforgiving servant, Jesus makes us painfully aware of the punishment for those who retain their anger and refuse to forgive. Jesus reserves one of his harshest criticisms and threat of punishment for this unforgiving servant. Jesus was the ultimate model of forgiveness and one of his last living acts was to forgive the thief who was crucified with him. After that, Jesus prayed for the forgiveness of all who had inflicted such hideous and cruel punishment on him.

This model of forgiveness was not lost on Jesus' followers. In the Acts of the Apostles we are introduced to Stephen, the proto-martyr, who imitates his Lord and Savior by forgiving those who are about to stone him.

Ultimately, the fact that we are Christians serves as the most powerful reason for being a forgiving person.

Reflection Questions

We offer the following questions to help in your reflection on forgiveness:

1) *Am I convinced that there is a spiritual and psychological value in becoming a more forgiving person?* Forgiveness is a prerequisite for becoming a life-filled and life-giving person. Explore the reasons why you believe it is important to grow in your capacity to forgive. What are the personal benefits for you in growing as a forgiving person?

2) *Am I ready to forgive myself?* Sometimes self-forgiveness is the most difficult level of forgiveness. Is your behavior self-penalizing? Do you punish yourself for those behaviors, thoughts and feelings that have never even surfaced to the level of consciousness? One of the most obvious indications that you have not forgiven yourself might be the lack of any joy in life. You might even believe that you do not have a right to happiness because you have not forgiven yourself for being less than the perfect person you desire and expect.

3) *Who are the people I must decide to forgive?* It does not usually take long to identify those whom you need to forgive. These people invoke a myriad of potent and painful feelings whenever you encounter them. Sometimes even a physical encounter is not necessary; all that is needed is to conjure up

the person in one's memory and the emotions come flooding. Memory is a powerful mechanism and one over which you have control, when you choose to exercise it. You are the ultimate projectionist of your own memories. You can choose to keep the images flowing or to shut them out. Imagery is a strong manufacturer of emotion. You can choose to recall either the pleasant or the painful experiences, and it is the memory of these experiences that determines whether pleasant or painful emotions float to the surface.

4) *Do I have a need to forgive God?*   Forgiving God is extremely difficult for many people. The ego ideal rebels at the very suggestion that you would actually be so angry at God as to need to forgive God. Even the thought of that may evoke guilt. Being able to admit anger toward God is a real sign of emotional and psychological maturity. Do you need to let go of your anger toward God? If you are able to do that, there will be freedom, relief and life.

5) *Who have been the models of forgiveness in my life?*   As you reflect on the significant people you have known, which ones leap into your mind as persons who have truly forgiven and, through their acts of forgiveness, have witnessed to you what it means to be a faithful follower of Jesus Christ? While these people have been very present and active in your life, you may have resisted even noticing them, since to do so would challenge you to change and to let go of revenge.

6) *Why do I continue to hold onto anger and resist forgiveness?*   The concept of secondary gain, as was explained, is operative in everyone. Until you are willing to admit that you *choose* to hold onto anger, you will find it difficult to forgive. At the heart of change is knowledge. Only when you can identify what gratifications and rewards there are, absurd as they may seem, will you have the freedom to choose the life that comes with forgiveness.

7) *Which beliefs or myths do I hold about anger that make forgiveness difficult?*   Immature, magical thinking often condemns a person to continued immaturity. Can you, perhaps with the help of a friend, identify some of your beliefs and convictions about this very ordinary, human emotion?

Attempting to undertake this task alone will probably not prove as fruitful.

8) *Do I pray for the gift of forgiveness?*   Do you, at times, forget that the ability to forgive is a gift of the Spirit? Do you dispose yourself to receiving that gift by praying for it? Do you often remind yourself of the frequency and unconditional love with which God constantly forgives you?

9) *Where in my life do I experience forgiveness?*   Sometimes recalling experiences of forgiveness and reliving the freedom and life that ensued can be the motivating factor to take the initiative to forgive once again. Recalling times of being forgiven can also help bring to memory the energizing effect this had on you, and can encourage you to be more forgiving in your life.

Forgiveness

MISCONCEPTIONS ABOUT FORGIVENESS

- forgiveness dissipates the feeling of anger
- forgiveness gives relief to the person forgiven
- forgiveness is only complete when I communicate it to the other

THERAPEUTIC ASPECTS OF FORGIVENESS

- forgiveness frees from painful memories and destructive impulses
- forgiveness helps to be creative and life-giving in relationships

REASONS FOR HOLDING ONTO ANGER

- protects from more painful and fearful emotions
- can protect from facing inadequacies
- protects from sadness and depression
- protects against intimacy
- gains attention
- controls others
- provides opportunity to wallow in self-pity

THE PROCESS OF FORGIVENESS

- cognitive conviction of need for forgiveness for own benefit
- attempt to understand the other
- desire for forgiveness
- choice to forgive

OBSTACLES TO FORGIVENESS

- inability or unwillingness to admit the anger felt
- inability to admit the need for forgiveness

- lack of adequate role models

- unrealistic expectations of others

INDICATIONS OF PROGRESS

- ability to express anger appropriately

- ability to ask for forgiveness

- freedom from fear and control of anger

- lessening of pain and anxiety

- ability to move into loving relationships

- admission of past hurts coupled with willingness to forgive

- realization that forgiveness may not dissipate the feeling

- experiencing pity, empathy or compassion for the other

Reflective Questions

1) Am I convinced that there is a spiritual and psychological value in becoming a more forgiving person?

2) Am I ready to forgive myself?

3) Who are the people I must decide to forgive?

4) Do I have a need to forgive God?

5) Who have been the models of forgiveness in my life?

6) Why do I continue to hold onto anger and resist forgiveness?

7) Which beliefs or myths do I hold about anger that make forgiveness difficult?

8) Do I pray for the gift of forgiveness?

9) Where in my life do I experience forgiveness?

Notes

[1] David C. Leege, "Parish Life Among the Leaders," *Notre Dame Study of Catholic Parish Life*, University of Notre Dame, Report No. 9, December, 1986.

[2] *Psychotherapy*, Vol. 23, No. 4, Winter, 1986.

[3] National Opinion Research Center, *The Catholic Priest in the United States: Sociological Investigations* (Washington, D.C.: United States Catholic Conference, 1972).

[4] *Redemptor Hominis*, No. 10.

[5] Frank G. Goble, *The Third Force: The Psychology of Abraham Maslow* (New York: Pocket Books, 1970).

Chapter Four

Self-Esteem:
The Path to Life

As we gathered to discuss our experiences of working with others to foster collaboration and community, we were amazed to discover how frequently our discussions centered around a single issue. It became clear that collaboration was most evident, successful and life-giving when the people attempting to minister together were individuals or groups who had a positive sense of self-esteem. Looking at the situation from the opposite point of view produced the same results: The major obstacles to collaboration were all related to self-esteem. The most frequently cited obstacles were anger, hostility, conflict, competitiveness and loss. Each of these issues has a direct relationship to self-esteem. One of the major causes of anger, as shown in chapter 1, is a threat to self-esteem. When self-esteem is low, hostility and competition are high. From our experience as we indicated in earlier writings,[1] as much as 95 percent of all conflict may be directly attributed to a threat to self-esteem. Whenever there is an experience of loss of any type, in relationships, security, status, role or physical capacities, there is usually a corresponding diminishment in self-esteem.

We discovered a similar phenomenon in our work with communities, whether parishes, small Christian communities or religious communities: The single, determining factor for success or failure was the level of self-esteem of the members of the community. When the climate fostered self-esteem, the community was life-giving and productive. When the climate was not conducive to, or threatened self-esteem, chaos and destructive conflict usually ensued. These resulted in morose, joyless and ineffective communities. The dynamics of growth or destruction are true for individual members of community as well as for entire communities: A group can have high or low self-esteem. This phenomenon is often evident among parishes, religious organizations and congregations.

For a while we thought that the almost exclusive focus on self-esteem might be too simplistic. However, continued study, observation, dialogue and discussion with other professionals, as well as feedback from workshop participants, reinforced our belief that the single most important issue to be addressed in fostering collaboration or community is self-esteem. Self-esteem, then, is a major issue in determining whether or not living together or working together is life-giving.

Basic Beliefs About Self-Esteem

There are a few basic beliefs and convictions that we hold about self-esteem. These form the basis for much of what we will offer in this chapter:

1. Self-esteem is a basic human need.

2. Self-esteem is essential for full growth in the Christian life.

3. Each person must ultimately accept responsibility for self-esteem: It is not based on whether, or how much, others esteem us.

4. Struggling to develop and maintain self-esteem is a universal human issue. It appears to be a significant issue for many people in ministry.

Self-Esteem as a Need

To put the discussion of self-esteem into context it is necessary to begin with the recognition that self-esteem is a need. In the pioneering work on needs conducted by Abraham Maslow,[2] self-esteem is placed at the top of his hierarchical pyramid. This final need must be met before achieving that rare status of the self-actualized person.

Simply stated, a human need is something absolutely essential for life and existence. When a need is not met, physical, emotional, spiritual or psychological sickness or death result. One might compare needs to the ingredients listed on the side of a cereal box, identifying the daily minimum requirements of vitamins and nutrients. Needs are similar. A person who does not receive the minimum requirements of such needs as security, safety, love and self-esteem cannot continue to exist, to grow, or to be life-giving. The person thus deprived becomes sluggish and lifeless.

One phenomenon that interferes with need fulfillment is the inability or personal resistance to admitting that one has needs. The professional, detailed studies of the priest sponsored by the National Conference of Catholic Bishops,[3] was conducted by some of the most competent and respected professionals in the area of psychology and sociology. One finding related to the issue of self-esteem. The study noted that one of the greatest problems of the priests studied was not being in touch with and accepting their needs. From our experience, that finding is not reserved for priests, but could include many others in ministry. Implications flowing from this are far-reaching. An inability to admit the presence of needs prevents a person from taking the necessary steps to have these needs met and, therefore, to grow. When needs are not met, a person remains incomplete, stunted and incapable of living the full Christian life.

Self-Esteem and Growth in the Christian Life

Self-esteem is essential for survival, and especially for growth as Christians. Christians have a threefold call: to holiness, to relationship and to ministry. Self-esteem is a key factor in growth in each of these three areas of the Christian vocation.

A key ingredient in a mature, life-giving spirituality is a basic esteem, or love, for oneself. Bernard of Clairvaux often reminded his monks that the love of God begins and ends with the love of oneself. When love for oneself is not present, it becomes difficult to pursue or maintain a relationship with God. Without this relationship it is impossible to live in a fully life-giving, ministerial way.

For most Christians the call to relationship is lived out within the context of some Christian community. One of the greatest obstacles to the building of positive relationships in community is competition. Competition is, in fact, often the antithesis of the Christian spirit. When a spirit of competition is prevalent, energy is directed toward finding ways of enhancing self at the expense of others. Rather than looking at how gifts can be complementary within community, the focus is on enhancing self. As we have stated at the beginning of this chapter, there is a direct inverse relationship between self-esteem and competition. Low self-esteem, leading to extreme competition, often militates against the growth of relationships in community.

While every Christian is called to ministry, the persons most truly free to respond to the needs of others in ministry are those with a high degree of self-esteem. The degree of self-esteem determines whether energy will be focused inwardly toward self or outwardly toward the needs of others.

Self-Esteem as a Personal Responsibility

Ultimately, no one can give or take self-esteem from another. Its very name implies that it is a quality reserved to the self. The control over self-esteem rests within each individual and is not determined by others or circumstances. Given this conviction, a person can no longer blame others for one's low self-esteem. In particular, significant people and experiences in the past cannot be blamed for low self-esteem in the present. When individuals claim to be victims of previous life experiences, it is because that is the passive role they have chosen. Each person is responsible for self.

Undoubtedly most people could identify certain individuals who are held in high esteem by numerous others. They may be held up as the models in areas of parenting, teaching, preaching, spirituality, gentleness or pastoral care. If self-esteem were determined by what others believed, these individuals would possess it in an extremely high degree. However, this is not necessarily so. What anyone or everyone believes about an individual does not necessarily determine what that person believes about himself or herself. Others can influence self-esteem, but they cannot determine it. The determination is only within the power and choice of the individual.

Although no one can give self-esteem to another, each person is capable of creating a climate that fosters or threatens that growth. For most persons self-esteem is a very fragile commodity, and the climate can have a powerful influence on how one eventually views self. It is in this area of developing favorable climates that Christians bear serious responsibility for one another.

Self-Esteem as a Universal and Religious Issue

Low self-esteem is not an issue reserved only for religiously oriented people. Many mental health professionals have indicated that self-esteem is one of the major issues they face in counseling or therapy.

While it is a universal issue, self-esteem is often more difficult for religiously oriented people. The more religiously oriented a person is, the more troublesome it may be to develop positive self-esteem. Later, when we discuss the dynamic that effects growth in self-esteem, we will explain this further. An informal survey of a number of mental health professionals concluded that a disproportionate number of their clients were Catholic and that poor self-image was a major contributing factor to their poor mental health.[4] Poor self-image can be compounded when individuals attempt to live out of an excessive, and at times obsessive and unbalanced, spirituality of perfectionism. When Christian formation in the home, parish, religious community or seminary has reinforced this perfectionistic attitude, it will further impinge on growth in this area. The high and overly demanding ideals internalized by Christians can be detrimental when not accompanied by compassionate reflection and critical judgment.

Examples of Low Self-Esteem

What does someone with low self-esteem look like? The answer is complex because people struggling with low self-esteem may display radically different behaviors. The following are some scenarios that can characterize low self-esteem.

One example is a high school teacher who manifests low self-esteem through her obsessive competitiveness. She always pushes her students to be first in any school competition. She does this because she acquires self-esteem from always being first, or vicariously experiences esteem and value through the success of her students. In ordinary conversation she attempts to impress others with her knowledge and accomplishments. Every game is the ultimate test, since winning is everything. This type of person is condemned to a life of low self-esteem, since the criteria of always being the first and the best are humanly impossible. The result of not achieving this unrealistic goal is often depression. Depression will drive the person into even greater competitiveness, creating a vicious self-defeating cycle.

The opposite extreme is seen in the man who is not only afraid to compete but even afraid to try. He suffers not from burn out but from rust out. His rule of life is never to fail. Therefore, he must avoid failure and risk at all costs. His prevailing model is to "stick to the tried and true," to what is safe, secure and sure. The fear of failure condemns him to a life of low self-esteem. He has little to value within himself for he rarely accomplishes anything. He does not believe that he is a good and valuable person for risking, regardless of the outcome. In these two cases we see that the single issue of low self-esteem can be expressed in seemingly contradictory behaviors.

Still another example of low self-esteem is found in people who use the norm of being right as the basis for self-esteem. When their self-esteem is low they have a powerful need to rationalize, to cover up even any semblance of being wrong. They are never at fault, even when their error is blatantly obvious to everyone else. Their capacity for rationalization has been so highly developed that they find no problem in projecting blame even on inanimate objects, as long as they believe that it exonerates them from any fault.

We heard the story of a man who had a reputation as a poor driver although he perceived himself as an exceptionally good driver. Any negative comments about his driving were immediately met with a strong, defensive reaction. After a series of accidents, he was overheard commenting, "This car is accident prone." The sad thing about people like this is that in attempting to bolster a sagging self-esteem, they appear foolish in the eyes of everyone around them. They perceive the ridicule and pity others feel toward them and this forces them to revert to even greater rationalizations and defenses. Their self-deception is obvious to everyone but themselves.

These are a few of the varied faces that low self-esteem can display. The larger question is how self-esteem can be raised.

Understanding the Dynamics of Self-Esteem

We encountered a group of parishioners who had attended a workshop on self-esteem. The workshop leader informed them that if they would but stand in front of the mirror every morning and repeat magical incantations, proclaiming their specialness to the face reflected in the mirror, they would have better self-esteem. Would that it were that simple! That sort of advice was probably as much good as the horoscope we recently read that promised an increase in self-esteem in return for a change in diet! Popular magazines or tabloid newspapers offer "quick-fix" solutions promising increased self-esteem if you follow carefully and meticulously their specific suggestions. If their claims were true, it would not be necessary to print further suggestions; yet these same newspapers and periodicals make countless dollars endlessly repeating these simplistic solutions.

How does self-esteem develop? We propose a model that at first glance might seem simple; however, it will be personally demanding. The model is:

SELF-KNOWLEDGE   +   SELF-ACCEPTANCE   =

SELF-LOVE AND SELF-ESTEEM

This equation is both challenging and, at times, anxiety producing.

Self-Knowledge

The starting point for all self-esteem is self-knowledge. How can people esteem and love themselves unless they first know themselves? One cannot love, value and esteem in a vacuum. There must be some object worthy of that esteem.

Some of the great saints of the church have suggested self-knowledge as a prerequisite for holiness. St. Teresa of Avila advised her followers that most of their trials and times of unrest came from the fact that they did not understand themselves. St. Catherine of Siena stated that self-knowledge and appreciation of oneself is fundamental to holiness.

On his deathbed a wise old rabbi summed up a lifetime of knowledge, passing on his simple wisdom in two rules for acquiring growth, "know thyself . . . and always doubt thy motivation." The essence of this wisdom is the realization that everyone is basically self-deceptive. For any person to presume possession of accurate self-knowledge is a sure sign of self-delusion. Within each person there is an unconscious, defensive dynamic that works hard to protect the human psyche against anxiety: the anxiety that would result from facing the complexity and, at times, deviousness of one's motivation.

All behavior is need-directed. To understand any behavior, there must be an understanding of the need behind it. Yet, if each person totally understood his or her motivation, anxiety would not be the only emotion experienced. Realizing that one's behavior is in many instances motivated by the selfish desire to satisfy one's needs could produce feelings of guilt and embarrassment, particularly since most people spend a great deal of energy in convincing self and others of the purity of their intentions and the nobility of their motivations. However, as the old rabbi discerned, motivation and behavior often have more to do with satisfying basic needs than with accomplishing the more lofty ideals most would like to believe serve as the basis for behavior.

In conducting a workshop on self-esteem, the emotional intensity of the participants became evident. We had distributed a rather simple questionnaire, similar to the one on page 107. We were surprised at the responses. Almost everyone who had filled out the questionnaire reported similar feelings. Some feared what they might discover about themselves. Others reported feeling anxious, without being able to attribute it to any one specific cause. Other workshop participants were clear that further reflection had helped them unearth the source of their anxiety. They reported some of their fears as follows: discovering that they might not be good or lovable; realizing that new insights would require them to either change or take greater responsibility; suspecting that additional knowledge would confirm their greatest fear, namely, that they had little to feel good about, value or esteem within themselves. The intensity should not have come as a surprise, for self-protection is a common phenomenon. Like any organism, an individual spends energy defending the self against knowledge that might necessitate change. A dynamic in the human psyche fears the knowledge and responsibility that will lead to change. Everyone feels comfortable and safe with the known, even when they don't like it. There is a familiar dynamic of people in counseling and therapy. While their verbalized goal is gaining self-knowledge, much of their energy is directed toward resisting self-knowledge and change. A major cause of anxiety is self-knowledge and a fear of coming to know myself as I truly am, stripped of all pretenses and masks. It is this fear that produced the anxiety in the workshop participants.

We have reservations about workshops that promise to provide individuals with self-knowledge in a quick, painless and consoling way. Participants emerge from these workshops with a tangible, simplistic, pigeonholed description of themselves, one acquired from completing a single questionnaire. No one test can plumb the diversity and complexity of a human being. In the search for the holy grail of self-knowledge, such simplistic solutions often do a great disservice. Overly simple solutions can serve as a defense against the difficult and painstaking work of overcoming the anxiety to undertake the far more fearful task of stripping away neat categories and searching for the real person within. This was evident in witnessing the stress produced in those workshop participants who were willing to do the difficult and soul-searching work of self-examination. Self-knowledge is not easily won.

Self-knowledge is the sine qua non of self-esteem. Self-knowledge is the major task at the stage of human development called identity.[5] Achieving a certain degree of identity is essential to grow in the self-knowledge that leads to self-esteem. According to one study[6] there is some question as to whether the majority of people in ministry have successfully navigated and resolved this stage of identity to the degree of successfully enhancing self-esteem.

Traditional theory places the development of self-esteem during the psycho sexual stage of identity. Recent theory suggests that in the case of women self-identity begins with the development of intimacy rather than identity.[7] The truth is probably found in both viewpoints. Self-knowledge is the result of personal introspection and the sharing with another that part of myself which I discover. Each one of these actions contributes to self-knowledge. It is the self I discover in introspection that I share with someone whom I can trust. In sharing the self I have discovered, and the dialogue that results, I come to a greater, fuller, more honest understanding of the person I am. It is the continued understanding and sharing of that self that leads to an ever-widening concept and knowledge of the self.

If the research is accurate, that many people in ministry are psychosexually underdeveloped, especially in the areas of identity and intimacy, it is incumbent on the formation personnel of lay people, religious and clergy to provide the opportunities for continued development in the two areas of identity and intimacy. Many and varied avenues can be taken to achieve this goal, such as the following:

1) opportunities for personal reflection that encourage the development of the capacity for intimacy;

2) gift discernment processes among people working or living together;

3) leadership modeling examples of reflective people, willing to risk the challenges of intimacy;

4) willingness to confront a type of formation in the past that focused excessively on faults and encouraged a sense of false humility and self-deprecation;

5) new models of formation that focus more on the positive, God-given qualities in each person;

6) fostering a climate of affirmation rather than self-condemnation.

A myth that inhabits the thinking of many people is that by the time an individual has reached a certain age, a corresponding psychosexual growth will have taken place. Unfortunately, physical and psychosexual growth do not necessarily occur at the same rate. Given one's personal history and unique experiences, maturation on the psycho sexual level may have been delayed. Certain issues such as identity and intimacy may not have been satisfactorily resolved, and some chronologically mature persons can find themselves stunted in other aspects of their personality.

Failure to develop one's capacity for personal introspection and mature identity often produces adolescent senior citizens.

Self-knowledge is not a once-and-for-all, time-limited task; it is an ongoing process. Each person grows and changes through aging and through new experiences. Self-discovery and self-knowledge are ever-present, ever-unfinished tasks.

We do not promote and encourage a personal introspection that could lead to narcissism, self-preoccupation and stunted growth. The ultimate goal is always to become a generative, other-centered, Christlike person. Continuous self-absorption and failure to move outside oneself is a sign of an arrested development that must be challenged.

Self-Acceptance

If self-knowledge is a difficult task, self-acceptance is even more so. The challenge of acquiring self-knowledge must be followed by accepting and embracing the newly discovered self. The story is told of a Rabbi Zusya, who burst into tears on his deathbed. Asked why, the old man replied, "When I am ushered into the presence of God, he won't ask why I wasn't Moses. After all, I'm not Moses. Nor will God ask why I wasn't Isaiah, because neither am I Isaiah. Why am I crying? Because God will ask, why on earth weren't you Zusya?" This is the question that each person must answer. The road to holiness is not in trying blindly to follow the virtuous path of another's footsteps, but in faithfulness to the acceptance of the uniqueness of the person that self-knowledge has revealed. This process of self-acceptance is more difficult than it first appears. In the process of arriving at self-acceptance, numerous snags and obstacles can be encountered.

A story recounted by a religious brother highlights the difficulty of this task. As a young man at the time of his profession, he recalls promising poverty, chastity and obedience as a lighted candle dripped wax down his trembling fingers. The superior general, in a deep, somber, frighteningly reverent voice promised "that if you keep these things, I promise you eternal life." He was ecstatic in that first flush of innocent, pristine fervor as he realized that all he would have to do to achieve eternal happiness in heaven was to keep those three vows *perfectly*. He recalls that it wasn't until months later that the sickening question began to dawn on him: If the reward for living the vows perfectly was eternal life, would his judgment for not living them perfectly be eternal death? After the initial fervor and idealism had subsided, he was faced with the frightening, uncomfortable reality that he would never live those ideals perfectly, but rather that he was engaged in a lifelong process of conversion.

This story describes the inherent difficulty of self-acceptance, the second dimension of the equation necessary for achieving self-esteem. When the norm for self-acceptance is too idealistic and perfectionistic, it becomes increasingly difficult to accept self as an incomplete, sinful, less-than-perfect being. As we have previously intimated, this attitude of perfectionism is most noticeable in religiously oriented people, and especially in those who have made a public profession of that commitment.

A primary reason for this difficulty in accepting one's flawed self is suggested in the writings of two Jesuit psychiatrists, James Gill[8] and Luigi Rulla.[9] We have diagramed the basic model:

EGO IDEAL OR IDEALIZED SELF	+	CONGRUITY WITH THIS IDEALIZED SELF	=	SELF-ESTEEM
the sum of all those values I have consciously or unconsciously internalized		the degree to which my feelings, thoughts, attitudes and behavior match these ideals		

Each person possesses an ego ideal or an idealized self composed of all the "shoulds" that have been consciously or unconsciously internalized during the course of life. The blueprint of what a little girl or boy should be is conveyed in messages and internalized during childhood. These messages provide norms by which to measure oneself such as "Good girls don't get dirty and don't fight"; "Real boys don't cry and don't play with dolls or skip rope"; "Good children always obey their parents (and elders and religious and clergy) and respect them (whether or not they behave in a way that earns and warrants that respect)."

As teenagers and adults the ego ideal continues to have expectations and ideals indiscriminately poured into it, filling it with models for eventual evaluation of self. "Good Christians never become angry or fight or speak ill of another." "Good Sisters (or Brothers or Fathers) of a particular congregation will always behave exactly and with the same zeal and self-annihilation as the foundress or founder." "A good priest is available 24 hours a day, seven days a week, and is all things to all people, in the manner of Jesus Christ."

Self-acceptance and ultimately self-esteem become increasingly difficult for good, religiously oriented people. The ego ideal stores an inordinate number of norms for behavior, thinking and feeling. Self-esteem develops in direct proportion to how closely a person can live the ego ideal. The norm by which one measures self is the consistency between lived values, behaviors, thoughts and feelings and the combined shoulds of the idealized self reflected in the ego ideal. Self-acceptance is difficult because the self one tries to accept is in sharp contrast to the ideal.

The ego ideal contains its own specialized psychological mechanism. Any time one thinks about doing something contrary to the ego ideal there will be a feeling of anxiety. Any time one actually behaves in a manner contrary to this ideal a guilty feeling follows. Given the fact that for many this mechanism is indeed a storehouse crammed with shoulds, it is easy to see why anxiety and guilt may be the primary feelings of many good, holy, religious people. It also becomes clear why these same good, holy people might have difficulty with self-esteem. It is difficult to feel good about and to esteem oneself when the criteria for judging that value and worth are too numerous, unrealistic and overly idealistic. Picture, if you will, a person with a radar scanning device constantly floating overhead. This device registers every thought, feeling and behavior and holds it up for evaluation. Is it any wonder, then, that positive self-esteem appears to be such a rare commodity?

At some point in life the ego ideal finds itself on a collision course with another phenomenon, the real self, or perhaps more accurately, the perceived self, not who we think we should be, but who we are.

Idealized Self	Perceived Self
Who we think we should be.	Who we are with all our imperfections.

A French philosopher has declared that "forty-plus is a merciless age and will not allow self-deception." Often it is at the vulnerable time of mid-life when one is confronted with physical as well as moral shortcomings. The reality that one has not achieved the idealized self hits home and the sobering admission that the ideal is unattainable must be faced.

There is an interesting dynamic that occurs at the time of this emotional, cognitive, psychological collision: Self-knowledge does not lead readily to self-acceptance. Self-knowledge releases the painful emotions of anxiety, pain, shame, guilt and disappointment, and often results in self-condemnation rather than self-acceptance. Instead of accepting and esteeming oneself as a good, lovable, though fallible human being, the tendency is to decry the person one has become.

In one country where the culture values egalitarianism, where everyone is believed to be equal in status, if anyone begins to rise in stature above the others, the normal, spontaneous reaction is to cut that person down. They refer to this attitude as "chopping down the tall poppies" and they refer to themselves as "knockers." Interestingly, when we first heard the description, we realized that it could be applied to many people in ministry. Ministers do not readily or generously affirm their peers. Instead, there seems to be an attitude of knocking, or criticizing and belittling. Why, among such virtuous people is there this ignoble tendency to be so fault-finding and hypercritical of other good people?

The dynamics of the ego ideal help make sense of this seeming paradox. Coming face to face with one's glaring inadequacies depresses the sense of self-esteem. In order to salvage a sagging, sinking self-esteem, one begins to compare oneself to others where the comparison will be favorable. Criticizing elevates one's lowered sense of self. From this perspective, knocking, criticizing and belittling makes good sense. It assists in meeting a basic life-giving need of self-esteem. It takes an enormous amount of psychic energy to continue maintaining one's identity in this way, but over time this defense becomes self-apparent. The growing awareness that one's behavior is contrary to that ever-present, evaluating ego ideal results in a devaluing of oneself.

This hypercritical attitude is prevalent in preteen and early teen years. Youths struggling with the developmental task of identity achieve it partially through knocking others and enhancing their esteem through favorable comparison. While one might condemn the cruelty of this behavior, it is understandable because it is a convoluted method for developing a sense of identity and achieving self-esteem. It is more difficult to be tolerant of this behavior when it is observed in adults who utilize the same belittling, criticizing and knocking to maintain their sense of self-esteem. In adults this behavior indicates that they are at the same psychosexual stage of development as the early adolescent.

While knocking is one defense employed when trying to avoid facing the real self, there are other responses and behaviors. Some people will simply give up, stop trying to live according to any pre-established values and choose to live in ways completely contrary to their former ego ideal. Still others, facing the painful reality of their own flawed, less than perfect reality, will become depressed.

Mature, insightful people will make other decisions. The first step in coping with the depressing reality of the real self as compared with the idealized self is to bring to consciousness those norms that exist in the ego ideal and to evaluate their merits according to one's beliefs and standards. Do I believe that it is wrong to fight or to experience conflict? Is it permissible for me to cry, and to not live up to someone else's sexual stereotype? Should I feel guilty because I don't respect some of the cruel, malicious ministers or old people I encounter? Do I believe that a physically or sexually abusive parent has a right to my undying love, affection and respect? Do I believe that it is appropriate to feel angry and believe that I am still okay if I don't behave in ways that are ideal and perfect all the time? Am I convinced that I will never be like those who have been held up as exemplars of the Christian life and that I am different from them with different gifts and limitations, and this does not detract one iota from my basic goodness? Am I convinced that it is not healthy to be always available to others and never to be concerned about my own needs?

These are the types of questions to be addressed. However, since much of what is contained in the ego ideal is unconscious, I must be aware of my beliefs before I can change them. This is difficult to do by oneself and may require the assistance of a good friend, spiritual director or counselor to raise to consciousness that which has been effectively buried. Once raised, it is imperative to examine those beliefs that control behavior and determine if they are indeed personal convictions and to cull out those that are self-destructive.

Another way to begin to understand these hidden motivations

is through reflecting on behavior that indicates one's motivating ideals. Because behavior is need-directed, reflecting on behavior, ideally with a trusted friend, will help to bring about a greater awareness of the underlying, often unconscious, values that guide behavior.

Ultimately, the goal is to arrive at a conscious decision to develop and accept a realistic ego ideal that is growth-producing and consonant with personal convictions. Convictions that have fostered overly idealistic, perfectionistic attitudes are especially pernicious and in need of reflection and assessment to bring about change. This is difficult but essential to achieving self-acceptance.

Norms for Self-Esteem

Doctor James Gill identified four principal scales upon which most people base their self-esteem: significance, competence, virtue and power.[10] To base self-esteem completely on any or all of these scales leaves a person with fragile self-esteem.

The norm of significance bases self-esteem on what others think, feel and believe. A priest developed a parish questionnaire to evaluate himself and the other members of the staff. One question asked for an evaluation of the pastor as a homilist. Almost 95 percent of the people responded positively to his homilies. Only 5 percent were mildly critical. Nevertheless, the pastor became depressed. His sense of self-esteem was based not only on what a few people whom he valued thought about him, but what everyone thought of him. His criterion was that he had to be significant to all, a no-win situation.

We spend a great amount of time conducting programs for clergy and have many opportunities to review various studies and surveys of diocesan clergy. It is disconcerting to discover how many of the clergy have relegated their own sense of value to their bishops. Again and again these studies show how significant the evaluation and approval of their bishop is in the lives of these men. They are searching for and crying out for acceptance and affirmation from the bishop. They experience a great frustration and blow to their self-esteem when he will not, or cannot, respond in the ways they desire. Perhaps this same need or desire exists in laity and members of religious congregations, but there is insufficient research to draw conclusions. We would suspect that many people base their value as persons on how significant they are perceived by authority figures.

A competent, compassionate colleague of ours was recently conducting a workshop and became aware of the fragility of basing self-esteem on the values of others. At the conclusion of the workshop, one of the participants approached with a well-documented list of things he had found objectionable. In most situations the workshop leader would have simply listened and calmly responded to the criticisms. Instead, she over-reacted in a rather hostile way. On reflection she became aware that she was allowing one evaluation to determine her perception of her value, worth and esteem. She realized that the intense hostility she displayed stemmed from low self-esteem, and she was not aware of the reasons for her vulnerability on that particular day. Whatever the reasons, the fact is that she allowed this total stranger to control her evaluation of herself.

In early childhood, self-esteem is developed in proportion to one's significance to others one admires and respects. However, self-esteem that remains rooted in the opinions and evaluations of others will continue to be fragile and will frequently leave one vulnerable to an inordinately strong desire to please these significant others. It is profitable to reflect on who the people are in your life whom you allow to determine your value and worth as a person.

The second scale for judging self-esteem is competence, and it is this scale that leaves people in ministry most vulnerable. Maintaining self-esteem through work and accomplishments can lead to committed, self-destructive workaholism.

For too long, models for ministry have been persons labeled as zealous, but in reality these are people who have been addicted to their work as a way of gaining esteem from others. They often live unbalanced, unhealthy lives, leading to illness and early death; they are psychological suicides.

Competence may provide the necessary self-esteem for a certain period in a person's life. However, almost every priest we know. who has left the active priesthood recently has been in his early 50s and each one has shared a story that is now almost predictable. The priest invested himself completely and obsessively in his work and this provided a certain amount of satisfaction for a time. Soon after he had entered his 50s, however, he began to experience what is described in an old Peggy Lee song: "Is that all there is?" He realized

that he needed more than work to give him life; he needed relationships. In many cases he found the fraternity of priests or the religious
community to which he belonged to be insipid and lifeless, more often sapping his energy than providing real friendship, intimacy and
life. He reached a point in his developmental life where competence
and success were insufficient to sustain him and provide the satisfaction and meaning he desired and needed.

This same phenomenon was described in an article written
years ago entitled "Despondence: Why We See It in Priests."[11] The
author, a priest-psychiatrist, described a phenomenon he had observed in a number of the priests he had seen in therapy. Like all
other human beings, these priests had a need for self-esteem. For
many of them, the basis for their self-esteem was the esteem in
which others held them and the affirmation that others gave them.
The problem, the author discovered, was that for many priests
(and probably for many people in ministry), they were affirmed
primarily for what they did, their accomplishments. They discovered that when one continues to be predictably competent and
productive, he or she is taken for granted and the affirmation
ceases. Having been conditioned to expect this praise as a result of
their competence and accomplishments, they began working
harder and longer, but without the desired response of affirmation. Tired, frustrated and feeling unappreciated, they entered
therapy. The sad reality is that many left the priesthood to marry
the first sensitive woman who valued them for who they were
rather than for what they did.

A number of people were born into families where a person
was valued almost exclusively for work. When these people entered church ministry, that same virtue of dedication to work
earned them affirmation. It mattered little that as a result of their
compulsive drive to be busy, their lives were not life-giving. What
did matter was the value and affirmation they received for the
hours spent in a classroom or hospital ward, or for the fact that
they were thought to be so "dedicated" that they never took time
for themselves to be nourished and reanimated.

When competence is the major criterion for self-esteem, a
predicament occurs when a person is faced with retirement or a
decreased ministerial role because of age or failing health. It is not
difficult to predict that such people will often experience severe depression when their one and only prop for esteem is removed.

Do I put too much emphasis for self-esteem on my work, my accomplishments, my competence? Do I affirm others for more than just accomplishments?

The third scale for measuring self-esteem is virtue. A religious brother recently shared his story. He was working in a parish where he was respected and idolized by all who knew him. He was a man committed to people, friendly, outgoing, compassionate, pastoral and deeply spiritual. He recounted how in the course of less than a year he regressed from this alive, vivacious person to become a brooding, withdrawn, depressed, ministerially ineffective person.

What caused the transformation? His story was a simple, yet profound one. Due to some stresses in the parish, he found himself reverting to occasional masturbation, an issue which had not been a problem since adolescence. Ingrained deeply in his ego ideal was the admonition that a good person, and certainly a good brother, doesn't masturbate, and if he does, he is evil and uncooperative with God's graces. In his own eyes he now viewed himself as a less holy person. Needless to say, his inability to live up to his perfectionistic ideal of virtue in this area was causing diminishment and near annihilation of his self-esteem, robbing him of his vitality and the parish of a dedicated minister.

When one's norms for acquiring virtue are too harsh or unremitting they are not a source of life but of death. Virtue must always be seen as an ideal toward which one strives. The innate value of the human person is not based on achieving the ideal but in continuing to strive for it.

Power is the final scale and norm for self-esteem. Some people value themselves because of the power they possess, especially power over others. Their sense of worth comes from the way others not only perceive them, but are influenced by them. Like the previous three criteria, this one also results in very fragile self-esteem: The moment others do not follow, one feels less good about self.

In the case of each of these four scales, the locus of control is primarily external. Any time the source of our self-esteem lies outside self and is dependent on others it will remain fragile. The more the locus of control is internal, based on criteria over which there is control, the less vulnerable will be self-esteem. In addition, self-esteem will also be less vulnerable when it is based on more than one criterion and when the criteria are focused on the present rather than the past.

The Vulnerability of Self-Esteem

Self-esteem is not something developed once and forever. It is fragile. There are situations that can threaten self-esteem and render it vulnerable. As indicated above, the more self-esteem is dependent on external criteria, the more vulnerable it is. In addition to the four criteria mentioned above there are a number of other factors and situations that contribute to that vulnerability: transitional periods, medical problems or hormonal imbalance and periods of crisis.

Transition, any move from the safe and secure into the uncertain, is often accompanied by a threat to the balance of one's self-esteem. The transition can be of many different types, including changes in ministry and psychosexual development.

After 25 years of successful teaching, a woman assumed a new role as principal. She knew she was a good teacher and had received a great deal of positive feedback from students, parents and other teachers about her competence. In fact, she had been the recipient of several state awards for superiority in her field. As a teacher she felt secure, competent and valued. She was unprepared, however, for what she was to experience as she moved into the new role. As soon as she became principal she reported feeling overwhelmed, terrified and incompetent. After a year's experience as principal, she could look back and see clearly how vulnerable her esteem was during this transition from the known to the unknown. Her experience is a common one. Transition of any nature usually leaves self-esteem shaky and vulnerable.

In working with formation programs, we have frequently encountered mature, self-assured people suddenly questioning everything about themselves when they moved into the challenging and unknown experience of a novitiate. When people find themselves in any intense group situation, regression normally occurs: They behave in ways that are well below their acquired level of psychosexual development. Regression is a normal, predictable dynamic. It occurs when one attempts, in an unconscious way, to use new, intense group situations to re-create and work through the unfinished developmental and relational issues from earlier life.

No group seems to experience more regression than those undergoing formation programs in religious communities, and the regression is as real for the formation director as it is for those being formed. Regression should not always be viewed negatively. There is regression in the service of the ego, when regression is recognized and made conscious. It can serve as the agenda for further growth and life. When regression is not recognized, it can lead to destructive conflict and chaos. During this transition period, when individuals become aware of less than mature behavior, they often find their level of self-esteem undermined.

Transition and separation from people and places affects self-esteem and is usually difficult for most people, but for different reasons.

If ministers have developed a role-related rather than a personalized identity, transition can have a traumatizing effect. Leaving that role will threaten their very identity and, therefore, their self-esteem. If a strong sense of identity has not been developed, any change and transition can be devastating. The more a person has achieved a sense of identity, the less vulnerable one's self-esteem will be at these times.

For others who have developed a capacity for intimacy, transition and separation is frightening. Inasmuch as self-esteem can be based partially or totally on acceptance by significant others, a change from a ministry represents a threat to that relationship and, therefore, to self-esteem.

Transition from one developmental stage to another can also produce a vulnerability and anxiety. At each developmental stage there is a major task to be accomplished. At the stage of identity, there is the task of determining who one is and deciding what one will do with that person called self who is evolving. Once one begins to be comfortable with this newly discovered self, there is an innate drive to move to the next stage of development, intimacy, and risk sharing that newly discovered self with another. Movement from the newly found security of identity to the risky level of intimacy, where one feels awkward and inadequate, is a transition that threatens self-esteem.

A number of people have remarked that they question self-esteem at times of physical affliction. There is a close, almost symbiotic bond between the body and the psyche. When there is a breakdown in the body, resulting in ill health, there will often be a corresponding breakdown in the level of self-esteem.

This body-psyche relationship seems most pronounced when

there is a change in body chemistry. In particular, women who experience hormonal imbalance during menstruation and menopause may find that these biological and chemical changes produce a corresponding vulnerability in self-esteem.

Any crisis in life challenges the level of one's esteem. Adults who are forced to place an elderly parent in a nursing home often feel a sense of guilt, as long-buried values and beliefs in the ego ideal are challenged. A good child "should always be willing to make whatever sacrifice is necessary to keep parents in the home and out of the nursing home" may be a refrain that re-echoes within the person during this period of crisis.

Research conducted by Richard Lazarus and reported in *Human Development*[12] identified the conditions that were the greatest predictors of stress. Those who are most likely to experience stress are those who seek to be in control of situations, look for approval all the time, do not accept criticism well, have difficulty exploring feelings and needs, and have trouble saying no and setting limits.

Stress is a physiological response and even a cursory examination of Dr. Lazarus' conditions shows a direct relationship between stress and self-esteem. Many achieve their sense of self-esteem exclusively, or to a great extent, in seeking to maintain control over people and situations. Those who require constant approval have probably become fixated on attaining their esteem from being valued and approved by everyone without differentiation. People with low self-esteem abhor criticism. Personal intrapsychic investigation is extremely threatening to those who possess little sense of identity. Individuals whose norm for self-esteem is competence and acceptance by others find it almost impossible to set limits on themselves.

In each of these cases, self-esteem has a direct relationship to the stress experienced within the body.

Recommendations

We offer the following recommendations as you attempt to become more life-giving by developing and deepening your self-esteem. We hope to avoid the simplistic solutions we condemned earlier. While the solutions we propose may look simple, we caution the reader that commitment to this advice will exact a personal price, but one well worth the anxiety, the fear and the will-power expended. The suggestions and recommendations will be clustered under three headings: develop positive attitudes, work at coming to know yourself more fully, and have the compassion toward yourself to accept yourself as you are.

Develop Proper Attitudes

1) *Are you convinced that self-esteem is essential for your growth as a person and a Christian?*   Accept the fact that self-esteem is a need, a need you share with every other member of the human race. Failure to attend to it will drain the very life within you. Make self-esteem a priority in your life and continue to do whatever is necessary to develop it. Don't apologize to yourself or anyone for having this or any need. Realize that self-esteem is a need you have, both as an individual and, in particular, as a Christian. Only by becoming a person with a positive self-esteem will you be able to live the full, holy, apostolic life to which you have been called by an all-loving God.

2) *Will you take responsibility for increasing self-esteem?* Accept the fact that only you have the ability to increase or lessen your self-esteem. Take responsibility for your own actions in this behalf and cease blaming others in the present or in the past for your lack of higher self-esteem.

3) *Are you convinced that self-esteem is a process characterized by probable peaks and valleys?*   Learn to become more comfortable with the fact that self-esteem is a developmental process that deepens only with decisive acts of the will, moving to action. In the course of this process, realize that there will be times and situations when this esteem will be more vulnerable. If possible, during these times seek advice and counsel to come to a better understanding of the personal dynamics occurring within you. By doing this, you will have more control over this dynamic in your life.

Know Yourself

1) *What actions are you taking to come to greater self-knowledge?*   The inscription over the Temple of Delphi states, "Know thyself." As one way of coming to that knowl-

edge, we would recommend spending a significant amount of time responding to the questions found in the self-esteem reflection paper on page 107. If, in the course of completing it, you begin to experience that uneasy feeling of anxiety, as did the participants in the workshop we described earlier, search out a friend, a confidant, a spiritual director, a support group—someone you trust—to explore the feeling and its causes. Ideally, share your responses with that trusted other. Self-knowledge is never achieved in a relational vacuum. It is always discovered within the context of intimacy. In discussing your responses to the questionnaire, pray for the openness and honesty to avoid the temptation of seeking the simple, safe, anxiety-diminishing responses, and try to search for the real answers, even if initially they cause pain or shame. Remember, the goal of this exercise is to help you develop greater knowledge of yourself.

2) *Whom do I trust enough to help me in this task of self-discovery?* As we mentioned above, you will come to know yourself more fully only when you can risk allowing another to know the person you are in the process of discovering.

3) *Am I aware of my positive qualities?* Since Christian formation in the past often stressed identifying and exorcising the negative aspects of self, you may have become obsessed with the part of self that is incomplete, lacking or negative. This attitude may require revamping and counterbalance. When have you taken time to inventory your positive qualities and your gifts? Spend time alone, or with others, cataloguing, proclaiming and celebrating those positive qualities that are God given and often the primary source for self-esteem.[13]

Accept Fully and Unconditionally the Person You Discover

1) *Am I willing to explore the deep recesses of my ego ideal?* There is a need to be an iconoclast, willing to question the long-held, deeply-ingrained beliefs, values and attitudes that I have embraced. Enter into the difficult but rewarding process of examining behavior as a way of coming to greater clarity and understanding about convictions and motivating values. We reiterate the suggestion that this not be

done in isolation but in relationship, for the rewards will be greater.

2) *Do I have realistic expectations and criteria for judging myself?*   Am I convinced that I am successful when I *try?* Trying to grow, to become more virtuous, to be loyal or faithful in relationships is what matters. It is not the attaining of a specific goal or task or hope that determines goodness or value or worth, but the willingness to continue striving to do what is believed as right. By stressing the concept of trying as the determining norm, failure assumes an entirely different perspective. You are not a failure when you do not achieve what you set out to do. You are a success because you had the courage to try. Perhaps like St. Paul's admission to the Philippians, you must also learn to say, "I do not claim that I have already succeeded or have already become perfect . . . (but) I . . . try" (Phil 3:12). The goal is to learn to continue trying and to stretch without exceeding unrealistic limits.

3) *Will I become a more affirming person?*   Recall that knocking, criticizing and belittling will not help you grow in the ways you desire but will ultimately decrease your esteem. Choose to relate to people differently. Becoming a more affirming person greatly influences how I feel about myself, as well as enhancing others' ability to see themselves more positively. People relating the development of their self-esteem will often note a number of occasions when they credit development to the affirming attitudes of friends and others who valued and esteemed them. How often do you affirm the people in your family, community or ministerial group?

Conclusion

The ultimate criteria for enhancing self-esteem is the realization that each person has been made, sustained and loved into being by an infinitely loving God, who has taught us that we are made in God's image. What greater reason could there be for esteeming oneself?

One of us recently had as a client in therapy one of the most physically attractive, beautiful women we have ever met. In addition to her natural, physical beauty, this woman was beautiful in every aspect of her being. Her reason for coming into therapy was that she could not see and, therefore, could not accept this beauty. We knew therapy had come its full course when during a session she commented, "I know now that I am a beautiful person." This is the task for each of us, to be able to say, "I am a beautiful person, loved by God and made in the image and likeness of God."

Self-Esteem

NORMS FOR SELF-ESTEEM
- significance
- competence
- virtue
- power

ISSUES THAT CONTRIBUTE TO THE VULNERABILITY
OF SELF-ESTEEM
- external, rather than internal, norms for judging self-esteem
- periods of transition
- medical problems
- hormonal imbalance
- crisis or stressful periods

Self-Esteem Reflection Paper

1. If you were to rate your self-esteem on a 1 (low) to 10 (high) scale, where would you rate yourself?
2. What criteria did you use to make that judgment?
3. Why do you believe that self-esteem is important?
4. When was your self-esteem the highest? What contributed to its being high? How did you behave when your self-esteem was high?
5. When was your self-esteem the lowest? What contributed to its being low? How did you behave when your self-esteem was low?
6. Can you identify a particular time or situation when your self-esteem seemed most vulnerable? What do you believe caused that? What did you learn about yourself from that situation?
7. Can you identify the major criteria upon which your self-esteem is based?
8. When your self-esteem is low, what do you do to help raise it?

Notes

[1] Loughlan Sofield, ST, and Carroll Juliano, SHCJ, *Collaborative Ministry: Skills and Guidelines* (Notre Dame, IN: Ave Maria Press, 1987).

[2] Frank G. Goble, *The Third Force: The Psychology of Abraham Maslow* (New York: Pocket Books, 1970).

[3] National Opinion Research Center, *The Catholic Priest in the United States: Sociological Investigations* (Washington, D.C.: United States Catholic Conference, 1972), and National Conference of Catholic Bishops Committee on Pastoral Research and Practices, *The Catholic Priest in the United States: Psychological Investigation by Eugene C. Kennedy and Victor J. Hechler* (Washington, D.C.: United States Catholic Conference, 1972).

[4] George J. Dyer, "Ten Questions From the Parish," *Chicago Studies*, Vol. 25, No. 3, November 1986, pp. 239-251.

[5] Erik Erikson, *Childhood and Society* (New York: Norton, 1963).

[6] National Opinion Research Center, *The Catholic Priest in the United States: Sociological Investigations* (Washington, D.C.: United States Catholic Conference, 1972).

[7] Simone de Beauvoir. *The Second Sex.* Translated by H.M.Parshley (New York: Vintage, 1974); Nancy Friday, *My Mother, Myself* (New York: Dell, 1977); Carol Gilligan, *In a Different Voice* (Cambridge, MA: Harvard University Press, 1983); Madonna Kolbenschlag, *Kiss Sleeping Beauty Good-Bye* (New York: Doubleday, 1979); Janet Ruffing, S.M., "Mother-Daughter Remnants in Religious Life," *Human Development*, Vol. 3, No. 2, Summer 1982, pp. 46-54; L. Ullmann, *Changing* (New York: Random House, 1977).

[8] James J. Gill, S.J., M.D., "Indispensable Self-Esteem," *Human Development*, Vol. I, No. 3, Fall, 1980.

[9] Luigi Rulla, *Depth Psychology and Vocation: a Psycho-Social Perspective* (Chicago: Loyola University Press, 1971).

[10] Gill, "Indispensable Self-Esteem," *Human Development*.

[11] James J. Gill, S.J., M.D., *Medical Insight*, December 1969.

[12] Gill, "Indispensable Self-Esteem," *Human Development*.

[13] William Burkert and Loughlan Sofield, "Unwrapping Your Gifts," *Human Development*, Vol. 7, No. 2, 1986.

Chapter Five

Dialogue: The Key to Growth

The call to be human, to be Christian, is essentially a call to witness to the love of God through love for one another. No one can struggle through life very long without realizing the need for others. It is difficult to fulfill the purpose of existence unless there are other persons to give love as well as to receive it. God created human beings to stand in meaningful relationships with one another and with God. Life-giving relationships do not come about automatically, nor are they easy. It is in living and interacting that human beings learn to deal with anger, to forgive, and to build and maintain the self-esteem that is vital to life-giving mission. Ultimately, the ability to love one another and work together, to be faithful to God's call, is only possible when persons can engage in dialogue with one another. Dialogue, therefore, is the key ingredient in the journey of growth.

Dialogue is the successful verbal exchange of thought and feeling between two or more persons who are able to be open with one another, whether that exchange is pleasant or the cause of conflict. It is a two-way process in which people discuss issues that concern them. It entails an oral exchange of sentiments, observations, opinions and ideas. Dialogue calls a person to be vulnerable, to engage in the process of self-disclosure and feedback. In dialogue defenses are put aside and one listens with the heart. In effect, the message is, "I care about you, about what you are saying, and I want to understand, even if I don't agree." Dialogue is the main tool for union.

Unfortunately, many people have unreal expectations about dialogue. Dialogue is often equated with conversation, the casual sharing of thoughts and ideas. The assumption is that merely by coming together people enter into relationships, communion and dialogue. The French have a good descriptive term for what dialogue is not: *Dialogue des sourds* or "dialogue of the deaf" refers to a discussion in which neither side understands or makes allowances for the point of view of the other. There is no instant dialogue. Dialogue goes beyond relationship and communication. It requires commitment, honesty and practice.

Dialogue does not happen in a vacuum but in relationships in which a sense of bonding or connectedness has developed. Relationship is a prerequisite to dialogue, but dialogue is more than relationship. Dialogue is a quality of communication that allows people to share not only the beauty that exists between them, but also the painful and tension-filled aspects of their relationship. Relationships can lead to dialogue, but relationships can also hinder and deter true dialogue.

True dialogue occurs within the context of a positive relationship, one that fosters trust, openness and vulnerability. Not all relationships are positive and constructive; some are destructive. If a level of dialogue in which people can truly grow is to be achieved, time must be spent in developing relationships that are strong enough to sustain potentially threatening dialogue.

Inasmuch as dialogue takes place within relationships, it will be helpful to explore some beliefs about relationships. Following this, some principles of dialogue will be presented. This will lead into the consideration of a four-stage model for achieving dialogue and seeing Jesus as a paradigm of this model. Finally, exercises and suggestions will be offered for moving through each of the stages leading to dialogue.

Beliefs About Relationships

Because relationships are a precondition for dialogue, it is imperative to explore one's beliefs about relationships. Two are proposed for reflection: Relationships are essential for growth; some relationships can be destructive.

Relationships Are Essential for Growth

Relationships are a need. In God's plan everyone is created as a social being with a need to interact with other human beings. This need for interaction is as essential as the need for food and the other necessities of life. One discovers oneself more completely in face-to-face interactions and side-by-side loving, learning and sharing brokenness and fragility. John Donne said it well: "No man is an island, each is a part of the continent; a part of the whole."[1] Self-discovery and growth are worked out in relationship.

The need for relationships is so strong that solitary confinement is considered a severe punishment. When so isolated, a person loses the desire or will to live. Relationships are essential for life and growth into personhood.

Growth does not occur in isolation but through interaction with others. How people interact is determined primarily by how they feel about themselves, their self-esteem. Feelings about self are influenced by the attitudes of significant persons and ultimately, as indicated in the previous chapter, by the ability to accept the discovered self. Acceptance of self makes it possible to let down the bars of self-defense and open self to others without fear of rejection. Self-acceptance is the foundation for self-esteem and, ultimately, healthy relationships.

When there is no sense of bonding through the experience of good relationships, feelings of low self-esteem can become a serious problem. Mental health exists to the extent that we can be aware of and deal with the interpersonal relationships occurring in life. Relationships provide the necessary information either to affirm others or challenge them to make changes in their behavior.

People who have not experienced being accepted and who are daily exposed to attitudes of disapproval and criticism often fail to develop the sense of being loved and valued as persons. Their low self-esteem severely impedes their capacity to relate. They fear being rejected and will often learn to mask limitations and withdraw from others into loneliness and isolation. Fearful persons erect walls or defenses to avoid facing the reality of situations they feel incompetent to handle. They may become people-pleasers, covering up hurt with superficial smiles that mask the anger and hostility flowing from their sense of rejection. To outsiders they may appear all sweetness and light, but the "sugar-cube" walls they put up are as effective as any in keeping others out and in maintaining their isolation and loneliness. People build walls to hide behind because they can not imagine that others can feel simple affection and good will toward them. Like the garden variety turtle, they hide under shells, withdrawn and safe. To venture out results in being vulnerable, but to remain inside is to starve for lack of human nurturance. Life and growth require the risk of relationships. To become alienated from others is to become a stranger to oneself. Without relationships with others, contact with the authentic self is lost.

A friend working in a nursing home shared with us the experience of one of the residents who had not spoken to anyone for three years. It was the woman's custom to sit on the sun deck day after day, just rocking. Our friend would also spend her 20-minute break each afternoon sitting on the sun deck. Usually the only chair available was next to the withdrawn woman. Our friend would sit there just relaxing and rocking. Neither of them ever talked to the other. Several months passed with this as a daily routine. One day, as was her custom, our friend took her place in the vacant rocking chair and started rocking. Another woman came to the sun deck, took a chair next to our friend, and began chatting with her. Suddenly, the "silent" woman sat bolt upright, and shouted, "Shut up. . . . You're interrupting us." Our friend was shocked to realize that in her daily rocking, just by her presence, she had established a relationship with the woman. The doctor, on hearing of her explosion, was delighted and began intensive therapy with her. Having established contact, this totally withdrawn woman was able at last to begin the long, slow journey back to health. The sense of being with another person, being in relationship, was the key to her recovery and growth.

This example of the nursing home resident illustrates the premise that personality can grow only as it is opened to others in relationships. Genuine relationships with others require the willingness to abandon defenses, to venture forth and to risk being known. As Walter Burghardt has stated: "The paradox is, the only way I can get my act together is not in isolation but in relation. I find my life in the measure that I am ready to risk it."[2]

Fully functioning persons recognize their need for relationships with others, but past experiences may have made them cautious and afraid to trust. Most people hide from others until they have some assurance that others will not hurt them. Entering into relationships presents real challenges to growth but there has to be an openness to permit this to happen.

Everyone brings to community, whether family, work or living situation, a dark side as well as a gift-giving side. Fears, frustrations, powerlessness, loneliness and conflicts are all present. Often persons have an ideal of what community "should" be and suffer disappointment when the actual experience does not live up to the dream. People can become so enamored of the dream that they reject the real community of daily interactions. The image of the ideal causes them to reject the actual reality that calls them to growth. They may have to divorce their dream of perfect relationships and recommit themselves to living with a community of real people who will disappoint them in not living up to their ideal or dream. They must accept the dark side of their companions in community and ministry just as they accept the dark side of themselves.

Communication in the real world of relationships has its positive side. Through dealing with others you may find in yourself strengths of which you have been unaware. You may discover in yourself forces and energies you need for ongoing life. Through others in this real world you are challenged to deal with and grow through the dark areas of yourself that you would rather ignore.

Without positive relationships neither growth nor life will occur. The challenge facing each person is to be willing to risk entering into those relationships in spite of the problems and dark sides which might be encountered.

Relationships Can Be Destructive or Growth-Producing

While relationships are a prerequisite for dialogue, not all relationships lead to dialogue. In addition to a desire for life and growth, people enter relationships for many reasons—for example, to avoid loneliness, to change another person, to take control of another's life, to fill a need for security. When expectations about a relationship are unrealistic, uncommunicated, unconscious or unreasonable, those involved can feel that they have been betrayed. Many people in today's society have experienced relationships that were far from satisfying and are therefore reluctant to become involved even for the sake of community or ministry.

Following are three prototypes of relationships that can develop. Two of these types would result in anger, frustration and destruction. The third type is constructive, one in which dialogue and life can flourish. Of course, there can be degrees of relationship along the continuum.

Type I—Over-Identification

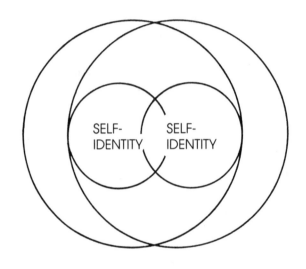

Overpowering relationship with consequent loss of personal uniqueness.

Type I is a relationship in which one or both persons over-identify. Usually one person overpowers the other with a consequent loss of personal uniqueness. There is relationship, there is communication but the egos merge to the degree where one or both persons fail to maintain their own sense of identity or personhood. This over-identification is destructive since it does not permit of the space necessary for dialogue. Some possible reasons for this type of relationship may be cited: an underdeveloped sense of personal responsibility, leading to a passive-dependent style of behavior; an exaggerated need for approval; a fear of conflict.

While this type of relationship is characteristic of childhood, it can have devastating consequences if it continues into adulthood. The dependent adult never fully develops. Potential creativity is condemned to atrophy: Energy is wasted; feelings of anger are suppressed, although these feelings frequently reappear in indirect hostility toward people and the world in general; dependency is developed as a way of life; self-esteem is diminished, lost in another more powerful personality. The overly dependent person ends up feeling victimized.

An example of this type might be found in someone living according to the old concept of "blind obedience." The perfect religious was so totally dedicated to carrying out the will of the superior that the person seemed unaware of any self-identity. The wish of the superior was the "holy will of God" and therefore was to be given primary consideration over any personal thoughts, wishes or desires. Those who were not submissive did not survive. One of our mentors, Angelo D'Agostino, a Jesuit psychiatrist, is quoted as saying that the pre-Vatican church generally attracted good obsessive-compulsive personalities, people who were often extremely submissive by nature.

Type II—Parallel Monologues

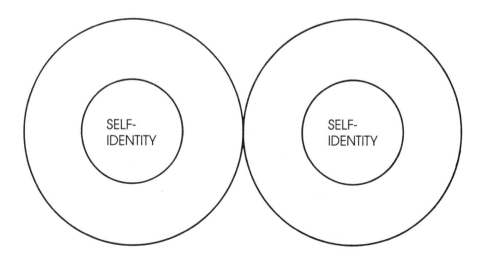

Relationship with no real communication.

In parallel monologues, people come together and take turns speaking, but no listening takes place. Each might just as well be talking to self. Neither person approaches the situation with the purpose of seeking the truth through sharing of ideas, sentiments, thoughts. There is no real encounter. They touch but they never connect. There is lots of talk but no dialogue, no messages *to* the one or *from* the other . . . ships passing in the night. Some persons have never experienced anything different from this. They might yearn for more but do not know how to go about it. A young man seeking help poured out his story. At the end he blurted, "I've never before experienced having someone really listen to me. Can I come back again?" It is sad to think that some people have never felt the relief of genuine dialogue.

Another example of this type of relationship is seen in the familiar parable of the blind men and the elephant. Without real comunication, each of the six blind men got a different picture of the elephant from experiencing only one part. And none of them was listening to the others:

And so these men of Indostan
Disputed loud and long,
Each in his own opinion
Exceeding stiff and strong.
Though each was partly in the right,
They all were in the wrong.[3]

Since people see only through the filter of their past experiences, no two see exactly the same thing. Each perceives reality as personally experienced. Conflict is therefore inevitable since experiences vary from person to person. Clarification through others is needed. The parable of the blind men illustrates what happens when judgments and conclusions are drawn based solely on one's personal experience. Can you think of times in your own life when this has happened?

The fact that these first two types of relationships are so common may account for much of the frustration and anger being experienced today. It is worth noting that in both of the types of relationships just described, there is a by-passing of gifts and talents, a crushing of self-esteem, a denial of the need for caring relationships. The three basic needs are violated:

1) to love and be loved,

2) to belong,

3) to be understood.

Often in the past to admit to any of these needs was looked upon as indulgence in selfishness or weakness and, for religious, a violation of the mortification to which they were expected to be committed by vow.

Type III—Dialogue

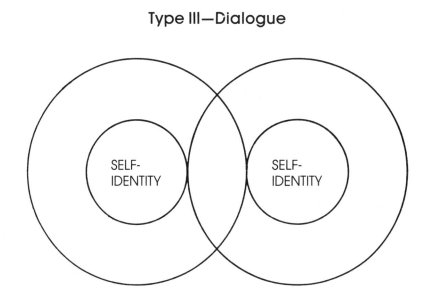

Relationship with real encounter and growth through sharing.

The third type of relationship might be called a dialogical relationship. In this relationship each person, while sharing, respects and listens to the other. The purpose of the exchange or encounter is to search for truth and recognize that each person may have some facts that, when shared, can lead to new insights into the whole situation or issue at hand.

This kind of relationship comes through a process of growth. It does not just happen. Some wit has put it well: "Minds are like parachutes. They only work when open." To be open to hear a position different from your own is always a risk. It requires maturity and a sense of self-esteem.

Principles of Dialogue

Dialogical relationships are an ideal toward which to work. Perfect understanding of one another will never be perfectly achieved, but this should not discourage people from striving toward the goal of experiencing genuine communication. The very effort exerted in striving for this level of relationship can be productive.

Some guidelines or rules will help develop more realistic expectations:

1) Tension is inevitable.
2) Dialogue requires maturity.
3) Dialogue is an art and a skill.
4) Dialogue develops through predictable stages.

Tension Is Inevitable

While dialogue creates a climate of bonding, tension will still be present because there is always diversity vs. commonality, uniqueness vs. sameness, separateness vs. bondedness, conflict vs. harmony, sensitivity vs. insensitivity, and differences of meanings, hopes, fears and understandings! Through dialogue and sharing, however, people become aware of each other's fragility, vulnerability and brokenness. This awareness helps them overcome fear of others and encourages effective dealing with tensions. Working through tensions is an absolute necessity if Christians are to be faithful to the common call to discipleship in Christ. Overt conflict can be avoided by engaging in a peace-at-any-price relationship, but this is really an injustice if persons are allowed to get by with totally unacceptable behavior. Genuine communities and healthy relationships challenge to growth, even when the result will be conflict.

Forming relationships in which dialogue can be realized takes time and involves risks. There can be no mutual bonds without a willingness to be vulnerable to other persons. Yet offering self to another person is the riskiest of all human endeavors because it places one in a position to be rejected by others. Before a person can enter into relationships this fear of rejection must be broken through. The higher the self-esteem, the easier it will be to run the risk of rejection entailed. Before a relationship can be established with another there must be some mutual knowledge, even though minimal. Self-disclosure cannot be forced or hurried. It can be a mutual adventure that builds progressively on previous revelations.

Self-disclosure is a means of building trust. It is difficult in our society because there is a kind of cultural ban on talking about self. It is a common phenomenon, though, that in a situation of anonymity, this restraint seems to be lifted. Have you ever sat next to someone on a plane or bus who revealed to you the most intimate details of his or her personal life? Without so much as an exchange of names, the person talks on about self. You might get the impression that you are hearing details even best friends don't know. Anonymity seems to let down the barriers usually imposed on us at a cultural level. When there is no risk there seems to be a greater willingness to share. Often a person has an idealized self-concept that can be presented to a stranger without the risk or fear of being challenged. The facade of anonymity is a protection. Often the self as conceptualized is not identical to the self as presented. Without a facade, the risk of personal rejection is high, so self-disclosure is avoided. In the anonymity of "passenger companionship" the protective mask can be dropped. So called self-disclosure to strangers is more like exhibitionism since it does not grow out of, nor result in, any real relatedness.

It would seem that dialogue should be quite naturally an everyday experience between persons who live or work together on a daily basis. Physical presence, however, is no guarantee of dialogical contact. In fact, the opposite may be closer to the fact. Persons living together can be miles apart in communication, in dialogical contact.

Dialogue Requires Maturity

One of the unreal assumptions made by adults working together is that "we are all mature people." The reality is that everyone needs to grow in maturity. The mature person, the fully developed person, is a hoped for yet never achieved ideal. Maturity is not a goal but rather a lifelong, ongoing process. Maturity is not an age but a state of being comfortable with self and therefore open to others. It is both a static and a dynamic concept, both a being and a becoming!

Maturity is the key to dialogue. It is an attitude of concern for others in daily encounters. The mature person has the gift for making others feel valued. This caring response is present whether or not we approve the behavior of the other. Acceptance is based on the worth and potential of the person as a creature made in the image and likeness of God. Initial acceptance of self is learned through the acceptance received from others. The mature person has a level of self-acceptance sufficient to encourage others to self-acceptance. This generates the trust that is basic to healthy relationships. Trust nourishes the person like oxygen and is just as necessary for life. Maturity presupposes an ability to give and receive trust. Without self-trust it is scarcely possible to trust another.

Mature persons accept their uniqueness as well as the uniqueness of others. Given this acceptance there can be open and unselfconscious communication based on respect for self and respect for the other. Defenses and masks are not needed for self-protection. Becoming a person in the fullest sense is possible only insofar as one can be accessible or open to others. Through the process of dialogue, self-identity is established through bringing self into harmony with others.

Mature persons recognize that their well-being is tied in with their ability to be continuously in touch with those about them, preserving their own identities and differences even while appreciating the otherness and integrity of their neighbors. Dialogue is undermined if persons are not mature enough to be comfortable and honest with one another, to refuse to use others or let themselves be used by others. This honesty or integrity is essential to maturity. Integrity is particularly necessary in the area of emotions as they affect daily living. The person of integrity, the mature person, has learned to respect and acknowledge emotions.

Emotions are special gifts of God. Concealing of emotions has become an art in our society. How often do you hear: "Control yourself," "You shouldn't be angry," "Don't cry." Many persons are embarrassed over expressing or even being witness to the expression of emotions. This negative attitude has grown out of a

Jansenistic distrust of human nature and has obscured the constructive element of the emotions in a life of genuine health and wholeness. Human beings are a psychosomatic unity: The mind and the body are indivisible. Spiritual and psychological growth must be worked out in the ordinary marketplace of everyday occupations and concerns. Feelings, externalized emotions, can be healthy and life-giving. Both love and anger are purifying emotions closely identified with daily actions and also required for developing spiritual growth. Both are basic elements of relationships and need to be recognized.

Emotions cannot be ignored. To hold emotion in check too rigidly and too long results in atrophy of the emotions. Emotions don't go away. They don't just go underground, they continue to influence behavior in subtle and uncontrolled ways. As a friend put it, "They continue to twist our guts." The person who claims to have no feelings or emotions often acts with coldness and is incapable of good feelings toward self, others or God.

Emotions denied have a way of being acted out. This is illustrated in a story related to us in which a woman, a teacher, confronted and challenged another teacher, a male, regarding his insensitivity to some of the students. She perceived him to be publicly humiliating the students. Following this confrontation the woman noticed a certain coldness in his behavior toward her. She approached him with concern and asked if there was a need for reconciliation. He seemed surprised and denied there was any problem; in fact, he assured her that he felt no anger toward her. In spite of this, it was apparent not only to the woman but to other teachers that he was acting toward her with anger and hostility. This usually took the form of indirect attacks on her at teachers' meetings. The man denied and repressed his anger, but the anger still twisted his guts and seeped out in his actions. Anger not admitted and talked out will be acted out.

Integrity requires openness in expressing emotions and in allowing others to express their emotions—a permissive climate in which others may truly be themselves. "Letting be" is crucial to integrity providing it is not an indication of indifference or apathy. Jesus was totally human in all things but sin. He experienced anger toward the Pharisees who watched him in the Temple, hoping for something to use against him. "Then he looked angrily around at them, grieved to find them so obstinate" (Mk 3:5-6). Jesus could show warmth, love and tears at Bethany over the death of Lazarus and the grief of Mary and Martha (Jn 11:33-36). Jesus was in touch with and comfortable with his emotions.

Dialogue: Art and Skill

Encountering persons and developing relationships which support dialogue takes both art and skill. This art and skill flow from the integrity of the mature person.

The art of dialogue has several elements: discipline, concentration, patience and recognition.

Discipline—Relationships must be nurtured with care, worked at. Securing and holding self-esteem and respect for others as well as for oneself requires self-control and commitment.

Concentration—Commitment must be of both thought and feeling. Relationships that support dialogue take time and attention. Many people are going in too many directions at the same time and end up being distracted and superficial. A genuine experience of dialogue comes only when one makes it the focus of one's attention, something deserving of the time and attention demanded. Developing a friendship is one illustration of this.

Patience—Self-disclosure and dialogue cannot be rushed. Growth and maturity in a relationship take time. In a technological society, "time is money." People are always in a hurry. Instant coffee, instant communication, my fax to yours!

Recognition—There needs to be a recognition of *you*, *me* and *us* in dialogue. This recognition requires faithfulness to self and to the other person. Dialogue may require sacrifice on your part, the giving up of some cherished opinion so that the truth may be found.

Dialogue is not only an art but also a skill. In addition to knowledge, there must be an ability to use this knowledge effectively and competently. There are many skills involved in the use of dialogue. Three of these will be discussed here because they are often so blatantly or conspicuously lacking in communication and relationships, and yet are so necessary if dialogue is to happen.

Giving criticism or confrontation.   There are times when criticism or confrontation is necessary. When this is the case, silence is not charity. The criticism, however, needs to be given in such a way as to be effective and constructive. In approaching any criticism, it is helpful to begin with the individual's strong points before calling attention to weaknesses or mistakes. This positive approach puts people in a more receptive frame of mind and assures them that their positive contributions are recognized and appreciated even while they are being criticized for perhaps minor faults and failings. It is useless to make repeated references to past failures or mistakes. This only results in the person's becoming resentful and defensive. The time and the place for giving criticism or confronting another is important. Public criticism or confrontation rarely serves any purpose since it forces the person under attack to indulge in face-saving and retaliatory behavior.

When Jesus cured the ten lepers and only one returned to express gratitude, Jesus criticized the nine who did not return. This objective criticism of failure was intended to teach others a lesson drawn from ingratitude (see Lk 17:17-19).

To give criticism or confront another in ways that are effective and promote dialogue requires both art and skill. Appropriate criticism and confrontation strengthen relationships. Criticism or confrontation poorly communicated blocks the development of dialogue no matter how well-intentioned the giver.

Saying no or setting limits.   Another skill in dialogue is the ability to say no, to set limits. Most people find this very difficult, since in general people like to be thought of as accommodating and nice. People experience anger and resentment when they feel imposed upon by others. Were they to go back over the scenario, they would find that they themselves are at least partially to blame for such imposition. A positive no at the beginning would have forestalled the accumulation of events or feelings of imposition. The difficulty in saying no appears to stem from an underlying fear of disapproval and hostility. As maturity in social relationships and dialogue grows, persons come to realize that others would respect a firm refusal far more than a grudging consent. Mature people recognize the right, as well as the obligation, to protect themselves from excessive demands on their time and energy. Limits must be set before others are allowed to develop expectations that are unrealistic.

Again, Christ, our model, had to deal with others' unrealistic expectations of him. In Matthew 20:20-28, the mother of Zebedee's sons came to Jesus with her sons asking something from him. "Promise that these two sons of mine may sit one at your right hand and the other at your left in your kingdom." The mother speaks for her sons but Jesus leaves no doubt in her mind. His response is immediate and to the point: "You shall drink my cup but as for seats at my right hand and my left, these are not mine to grant." No equivocation. The case is closed!

Taking a stance for beliefs.   At times integrity requires taking a stand for beliefs even when it means antagonizing others. Sometimes it is possible to be so intent on being "all things to all people" that issues are evaded or straddled rather than faced head on. Fear of misunderstanding and rejection arouse anxiety, yet truthfulness with others reveals confidence in their integrity as well as our own. To show faith in the ability to look at all the facts, objectively seeking to face the issue realistically, indicates trust. To violate the integrity of others is to lose sight of self and others as unique persons, with unique feelings, capacities and relationships. This results in barriers that affect relationships and interfere with dialogue. Jesus takes a stance against the Pharisees when the disciples are hungry and begin to pluck the ears of corn to eat. Jesus runs amuck of the Pharisees for not correcting his disciples for doing what is not permitted on the Sabbath day. Jesus defends the hungry disciples. He makes his stance clear. Human needs take precedence over all other claims (see Mt 12:1-8).

Dialogue Develops Through Predictable Stages

Just as people in general like to assume that they are mature, they also assume that all adults operate on a level of dialogue whenever they converse. Dialogue is more than just conversation. The implication for people living or ministering together is that until they have spent time discovering and accepting the self, revealing this discovered self to one another and discussing that private, sacramental area of faith experiences, there will not be an ability to dialogue about the difficult issues encountered in life.

The aim of dialogue is more than just to convince people. Its aim is to be understood by all and to understand the other persons. Communication becomes dialogue only gradually. It calls us to be vulnerable, to engage in the processes of self-disclosure and feedback. It is a developmental process. There are stages to work through before arriving at a point where differences can be openly expressed without raising walls of defenses. Good will is not enough. It has already been pointed out that dialogue is an art and a skill requiring maturity, that is, honesty and self-acceptance.

Developing Stages of Dialogue

LEVELS	GOALS	TASKS	FEARS	VIRTUES
I. SELF-ACCEPTANCE	To come to a deeper understanding of who I am	Spend time in personal reflection	Self-knowledge	Humility
II. SELF-REVELATION	To risk vulnerability and self-revelation	Disclose to others aspects of self I have discovered	Rejection	Trust
III. FAITH SHARING	To share faith	Share personal experiences of God	Ridicule	Serenity
IV. DIALOGUE	To experience genuine communication	Risk discussing difficult issues	Destruction of self or group	Courage

Dialogue builds through stages. We therefore present a four-stage model indicating the steps that lead to dialogue. Each level has its own goals, tasks, fears and virtues. Each builds on the previous levels.

A Four-Level Model for Development of Dialogue

Each level or stage will be discussed. At the end of the chapter suggestions will be made for exercises that can be used to achieve the goal for each level. Dialogue is not easy but the results for community and ministry are well worth the effort.

Level One: Self-Acceptance. The goal of this level is to come to a deeper understanding of who I am.

Self-knowledge is a prerequisite for self-acceptance. Without self-knowledge a person cannot grasp either personal giftedness or personal limitations. There is a tendency to exaggerate faults and consequently to give in to discouragement and to project weaknesses on others, resulting in deafness to God's call. Self-knowledge and self-acceptance are difficult to acquire. It takes courage and humility to sift down to insights about self that one would rather not face. The light of the Holy Spirit as well as recourse to the model of Christ are needed.

The first level develops as people begin to accept the truth of their personal goodness and the fact of their abilities and their talents, as well as their weaknesses and liabilities. With humility the person says, "This is me." Once self has been accepted, the person can afford to let down the bars of defensiveness and be open to others without fear of rejection. Acceptance of self requires humility which is the foundation of healthy relationships. Self-knowledge and self-love open the person to loving others as well as self. When self is not accepted the person is unable or unwilling to accept others, that is, to move to the next level of risk and vulnerability.

Level Two: Self-revelation. The goal is to risk vulnerability and self-revelation. This is when one learns to disclose the discovered self.

This level flows from and builds on the first level. When I have accepted the self that I am, I can begin to risk telling others about myself, to engage in self-disclosure regarding some aspects of the self I have discovered. I come to a freedom to express my feelings even when they are different from those of others. At this level I may wish to tell my story, the story of how I came to be where I am.

I will still experience some vulnerability and anxiety. I may still keep large areas of myself private and unshared, but I have begun the process of letting others know me. This opening of myself allows me to experience caring and listening from others. Others may begin to give me feedback about myself which can lead to the next level of interaction.

Level Three: Faith Sharing. The goal is to share faith.

Sharing feels more comfortable. People are free to use their energies in constructive ways of their own choosing rather than trying to meet expectations of others. The most important attitude now is to get in touch with what God is asking based on all the experiences up to this point in life.

Different persons will progress at different rates at this level of sharing. Sharing cannot be forced or hurried. It should be allowed to proceed at a rate comfortable for each person. Growth is always tempered by the background of the individual. At this stage a person begins to be able to shake off some of the shoulds and oughts of expectations that have been internalized. As one is able to articulate how God has been at work in one's life, new insights into one's spirituality are discovered. Hearing others' experiences is a source of encouragement and edification, which energizes the Christian and results in growth in faith. Often as they engage in faith sharing, persons experience a sense of the nearness of God's presence in themselves as well as in others.

Level Four: Dialogue. The goal is to experience genuine communication. This will always remain a process rather than an accomplished goal.

Persons can begin to risk discussing issues of communal importance. At this level anger and conflict become elements for growth rather than destructive and frustrating experiences. Feelings are more likely to be explored honestly, even while differences exist over opinions and issues. Individuals can hear each other without experiencing a sense of win-lose. Listening is of major importance in dialogue. Listening is more than hearing with the ears. Listening and hearing are not identical. Hearing refers to the actual perception of sound while listening refers to the attachment of meaning to the auditory symbols perceived. Listening is what we hear, understand and remember.

Sometimes it seems as if we talk and think we have all the answers, but when we reflect we know something is lacking. Learning to dialogue is something like learning to ride a bike. Remember how simple it seemed when you watched your big brother or sister ride? When they finally agreed to teach you, you wondered why they didn't just let you get on and go! Turning pedals seemed so simple, so obvious. Nothing to it! The actuality was a bit different. No one could explain to you about a very simple but basic factor— balance! Only experience and practice could fill the gap.

Each person can go through the stages of reading about dialogue and the steps needed to acquire the art and skill. However, these guidelines and rules must be experienced, practiced and mastered, just like balancing on a bicycle. When you know how, it can become a challenging and positive experience. Proficiency comes with practice.

While monologue isolates a person, dialogue opens ways to real contact between people, to mutual understanding at deeper levels. If we believe deeply in our ministry and community, our faith will enable us to muster the forces, the energy and the commitment necessary to master the art of dialogue.

The word *dialogue* is loosely used in everyday speech. It is, therefore, not to be wondered at that persons speak of dialoguing when, strictly speaking, they have merely exchanged a few superficial words with another. Dialogue is a progressive development of relationships between self and others requiring appropriate communication skills at each level. Persons who expect dialogue on a first encounter are doomed to frustration and disappointment.

To relate to one another on the level of dialogue is challenging, but we have a model to guide us. Christ has come to show us how to respond to our call to be in relation with God and one another. He is our principal model for he has said: "I am the Way; I am the Truth and Life" (Jn 14:6). In studying the paradigm of Christ we come to the essence of our call to work and live together, to challenge one another to growth through dialogue.

Jesus: The Paradigm for Dialogue

1. **Climate**

   His actions and words first create a climate where growth and inner healing can take place.

2. **Compassionate Perception**

   He sees people with problems rather than problem people.

3. **Personal Response**

   He responds to people where they are—physically, emotionally, spiritually, whatever their need.

4. **Relationship**

   He risks entering into relationships with others, shares himself with them and invites them to live and to grow.

5. **Dialogue**

   He confronts them with their weaknesses but calls them to life and growth.

Dialogue is the dynamic that Christ used. Day in and day out Christ was there with the people, teaching them and listening to them. He created a climate of trust. He spoke to them concerning the gut issues of their lives. He knew the problems facing them. He was concerned about their concerns. Yet he did not hesitate to confront them, to criticize when criticism or confrontation seemed indicated. He revealed himself to them. He dialogued.

We will take one of the many examples in the life of Christ to see how he modeled dialogue.

The Samaritan Woman at the Well (Jn 4:4-20)

1. *Jesus creates a climate.*   Jesus does the unexpected. He greets this Samaritan with a courtesy not usually found between Jews and Samaritans. Not only is she a Samaritan but she is a woman. A climate for a relationship is set up.

2. *Jesus reveals a compassionate perception of the person before him.*   Others from the village may see her as a "loose woman." Christ sees her as a woman alone, hurting and confused and leads her into a conversation about herself.

3. *Jesus makes a personal response to her hurt.*   He does not condemn her, but accepts her and forgives her even before she asks for forgiveness. He reveals to her his own identity.

4. *Jesus initiates a relationship with her.*   Having begun communicating with her, he leads her from fear to real listening, to questioning, to sharing her beliefs.

5. *Jesus confronts her with her lack of commitment.*   His concern arouses in her a sense of life and receptivity to his message. His confrontation lifts a burden from her shoulders. She has risked herself in this encounter and Jesus has met her on the same level, the level of dialogue, of genuine communication.

Only after Jesus has established a relationship with the Samaritan woman is he able to enter into dialogue with her. The same is true for us.

Summary

Dialogue is a product of constructive relationships in which people have achieved self-knowledge, self-esteem and maturity sufficient to permit exchanges of thoughts, feelings and ideas without sacrificing their own values or moral codes. These exchanges are verbal.

Dialogue is the fruit of previous levels of growth. Dialogue entails movement toward mutual understanding. It calls human beings to fullness of life through vulnerability to one another in order to achieve life in the Spirit. It is the capstone of life together, requiring courage to risk letting others into one's private space beyond what each would like to be, and into what one really is. It calls for honesty in expressing oneself even when this involves giving criticism, setting limits or standing for one's belief or values or moral code.

People in dialogue:

—try to receive feelings and thoughts of others without attempting to change them;

—can let others be themselves even when they are different;

—listen without trying to refute or argue down the speaker;

—listen to understand;

—ask questions to check out or insure understanding;

—don't sit in judgment;

—are open to being changed should the evidence point in this direction.

Dialogue moves a relationship from dependence to interdependence, to a sense of belonging and bonding to the life-giving relationships for which human beings are created. Through these life-giving relationships dialogue becomes the key to growth.

We now present suggestions and exercises to be used in working through the four stages, always keeping in mind that dialogue is an ongoing process, never completely accomplished, always moving toward the goal.

Exercises For Achieving Dialogue

The exercises which follow are based on this model:

Developing Stages of Dialogue

LEVELS	GOALS	TASKS	FEARS	VIRTUES
I. SELF-ACCEPTANCE	To come to a deeper understanding of who I am	Spend time in personal reflection	Self-knowledge	Humility
II. SELF-REVELATION	To risk vulnerability and self-revelation	Disclose to others aspects of the self discovered	Rejection	Trust
III. FAITH SHARING	To share faith	Share personal experiences of God	Ridicule	Serenity
IV. DIALOGUE	To experience genuine communication	Risk discussing difficult issues	Destruction of self or group	Courage

A Four-Level Model for Development of Dialogue

Introduction

For each of the levels in this model, exercises have been suggested for growth at that stage. Within each level there is no particular sequence to be followed. Persons or groups can select whatever exercise will be helpful in their particular circumstance or suited to their particular needs. The levels themselves are sequential. Each builds on the previous level. A person or group may choose to repeat certain exercises or choose to skip around within the level. It is suggested that sufficient time be given to reach the goal for each level before proceeding to the next level.

LEVEL I: SELF-ACCEPTANCE

GOAL: To come to a deeper understanding of who I am
TASK: Spend time in personal refection
FEAR: Self-knowledge
VIRTUE: Humility

In these exercises be yourself at your deepest level. Try to move from the impersonal, from playing a role, to the personal, to living your own uniqueness, your own time and place, reflecting on the gifts you have, the person you are with God. Talk with God about who you are and who you want to be. Savor the mystery of your existence as a child made in the image and likeness of God.

Where is God calling you to be right now? Let down your defenses and allow God to lead you to places you never thought to go. Let God unmask you and lead you gently.

Reflections at this level are not for sharing at this time. They are just for yourself to help you experience the love of God so that you can come to an acceptance of the self God knows and loves.

1. *Reflection:* Myself as mystery

   "I have called you by your name, you are mine" (Is 43:1-4).

   "Yes, I know what plans I have in mind for you, Yahweh declares" (Jer 29:11).

   —How is God calling me? What might be the special name by which I am called? What would I like to be called? Why?

   —Who are the people in my life who have loved me, cared for me, who are responsible for my being where I am today?

   —Take time to reflect on those relationships. What do they tell me about myself?

   —What surprises have I had in my life, what unexpected turning points?

   —As I reflect on them now, how did they affect the person I am today?

   —I imagine myself standing before the face of God. What do I want to say to God now? God's choice of me is eternal, but it must be ratified by my response in time. This can be done only gradually over the course of my life. I cannot pledge God my fidelity but I can pledge my effort to grow in fidelity.

—When have I been aware of God's holding me in the palm of God's hand? Remember. Believe. Recall. Do I trust God? Do I believe in the loving care of God for me?

—Can I recognize God's caring plans for me in my daily life? Where and in what specific ways?

—Ask God's help in bringing you to greater self-knowledge and self-love.

2. *Reflection:*   My present reality before God

"Yahweh, you examine me and you know me" (Ps 139:1).

—I imagine a line stretching from my birth to my death.

Where am I now in regard to this line?

What does it feel like to have God touching me tenderly, probing me?

How does it feel to be held in the palm of God's hand?

Am I responding to God now as I wish to respond?

Are there any things in my life which I would like to change so that God can work more effectively in me?

What are they?

—Be gentle with yourself as you rest in God's love.

3. *Reflection:*   Who am I?

—What insights have I gained about myself through the above reflections?

Can I put these insights into words?

What do I fear having others know about me?

—Imagine you are about to meet someone important for the first time. This person knows nothing about you and you want to give them a genuine picture of yourself . . . the real you. You have only a few minutes to do this. You will have time for no more than 17 words; use fewer if possible. You may use a metaphor, for example, a rose bush, a clay vessel, an early morning cloud, or you may use something like John the Baptist did: "I am the voice of one crying in the wilderness, make straight the way of the Lord."

4. *Reflection*:   Self-examination on communication

Listening: How well do I really listen?

—For instance, when someone tells me that they have just returned from vacation, what is my response? Do I tell them what I have been doing or do I ask them to share with me what the experience was like for them?

—When someone expresses anger toward me, do I try to be sensitive to their feeling? Do I recognize when they are scared, hurt or confused?

—Do I really want to hear what others are saying, or is there something going on inside me that defends me from really hearing?

—When someone is speaking to me, I try to imagine that it is God. What kind of presence would I want to give God? What does this tell me about myself?

Responding:

—When did I leave an encounter with someone and feel good about what had transpired? What was going on within me to make this possible? When I reflect on it now, what do I think the other person was doing that facilitated this climate?

—Do I often leave meetings or encounters with others feeling frustrated over not having communicated what I was feeling? What kept me from saying what I wanted to say?

—I call to mind situations in which I felt comfortable and at ease; or uncomfortable and wanted to get out. What made the difference?

Self-Disclosure:

—How willing am I to let others know me?

—What is the worst thing that could happen if I allowed others to look behind my "mask"?

—What fears keep me inside myself?

LEVEL II: SELF-REVELATION

GOAL: To risk vulnerability and self-revelation

TASK: To disclose to others aspects of the self I have discovered

FEAR: Rejection

VIRTUE: Trust

No one can know us unless we are willing and able to tell them who we are through our actions, words and gestures. Loneliness and misunderstanding arise from our inability to present ourselves honestly in our encounters with others.

At Level II the sharing is short and simple. What we reveal is limited to nonthreatening material. The purpose is to build up trust gradually so that a *climate* of trust begins to be present. Trust begets trust! As sharing progresses, it is most important that we listen intently to one another, valuing differences and respecting the vulnerability and fragility of each person. For some this sharing will be a new experience and may be difficult. Respect and confidentiality is a must if trust is to prevail.

Sharing is at the level where one is comfortable. This will vary from person to person.

At this point it may be helpful for individuals to share their fears or expectations of what is to happen. This sharing may be between just two people or a small group of people who choose to get together. The most important point is that the person sharing feels safe and comfortable.

Sharing:

Share with another or others the 17 words you wrote describing the essential you in the above exercise. Sharing these words can generate strong positive feelings among those sharing.

Scriptural passage:

Select a favorite scriptural passage, a passage that has sustained you in time of trial or sorrow, or a passage that seems to sum up and express something important for you.

Whatever passage you choose, share what makes it meaningful for you.

My story:

In a straightforward and simple way tell the facts of your life. This is a short account of no more than five to ten minutes. It can include anything you think "explains" who you are to others. It may be humorous, sad, whatever.

LEVEL III: FAITH SHARING

GOAL: To share our faith lives
TASK: To share personal experiences of God
FEAR: Ridicule
VIRTUE: Serenity

Faith sharing as we are using it here refers to the way in which we communicate our personal experiences of and responses to Jesus Christ. I let others know what is happening in me at this deepest level of relationship. I am the only one who knows what is going on in me and I share it with another person or group. I choose to share this because of my conviction that we are called together in Christian relationship and community to share at this level of faith so that we can grow more fully in our relationship with our God.

As a result of this sharing, we grow together in communion in Christ. Each of us lives a spiritual life from our own unique center as elevated by grace. What we feel, perceive, imagine, will or do, comes into being from the core of our own uniqueness where we personally meet Christ as he reveals himself in our daily lives. This is our spiritual world of meaning. In order to use this core faith experience, I have to look back over my life and raise the experience to the level of awareness so that I can use it consciously in living out my Christian life and ministry.

Faith sharing began when God gave us Jesus Christ, the Word, to reveal to us a personal God. This sharing reached its climax at the discourse at the Last Supper. Christ told his apostles of his life in the Trinity. Faith sharing is a long tradition beginning with Christ and his disciples. The gospels are the faith sharing of the evangelists, their reactions to Christ, the details of their lives with Christ. Paul also tells us of his personal experiences with Christ, of his fears, his anxieties, hopes and love for Christ. Other examples of faith sharing are the *Confessions* of St. Augustine and the autobiographies of St. Ignatius, St. Teresa of Avila and St. Therese of Lisieux.

Your own personal experience of God comes about at the level of your own inner feelings, thoughts and images. Through verbal description or articulation you can help other persons to "experience" your experiences of the Lord. This kind of sharing strengthens the bonding in Christ. Faith sharing is a more profound, and therefore riskier, sharing than the sharing at the second level.

Faith Sharing: Where have I personally met the Lord being revealed through my daily life from *birth* to *now*?

Sharing takes place in consecutive sessions with the same person or persons. If there are several persons sharing it will be better to separate the sessions so that participants do not get tired. This kind of listening is intense and can be tiring, yet attentive listening is of utmost importance. Short breaks can be beneficial, and should be provided as seems appropriate.

Each segment is introduced with an appropriate scriptural reading. This is read aloud. The readings suggested are intended to provide a setting or background for Christian sharing, since the goal of faith sharing is to deepen faith and bonding in Christ. Faith sharing sessions are not therapy sessions.

The place selected for faith sharing should be free of distractions and fairly quiet to allow for a reflective mood to prevail. It is imperative that each person be heard when speaking. There seems to be a natural tendency to lower one's voice when speaking of things sacred. People may have to be reminded to speak clearly and audibly. Sharing should not be hurried; people speak as they are ready.

Session 1   —   First religious experiences up to late childhood.

Reading: Philippians 2:1-5 or 1 Corinthians 1:4-9

Content of session:

—first encounters with God through people

—experiences as a child where God first entered your awareness

—how you first became aware of God's call to ministry and how you responded to that call

—family experiences that contributed to your response to ministry/community service

Session 2   —   Religious experiences from early years of school up to the present time

Readings: Isaiah 43:1-5 or Proverbs 22:17-19

Content of Session:

—Christ alive in you and through you; writing your contemporary testament just as the evangelists wrote their testaments

—the joys, sorrows and crises through which God has brought you to where you are now, has touched your life and called you to witness to Christ

Session 3   —   Personal reflection on God's goodness to you, followed by sharing these reflections

Readings: Jeremiah 18:1-7 or Isaiah 64:8

Content of Session:

—personal reflection on the presence of God as you have experienced it through your personal memories and through listening to others with whom you have been sharing

—How has the "potter" been at work in shaping the clay of your life?

—Try to synthesize all you have experienced during these sharing sessions.

Session 4   —   Sharing who is Christ to you

Reading: Matthew 16:13

Content of Session:

—Imagine Christ addressing to you the question he asked Peter: "Who do you say that I am?"

—Reflect on how you would answer this question addressed to you.

—Share your response with others.

Session 5   —   Sharing how each person sees the seal of Christ in the other people present

Reading: 2 Corinthians 3:2-3

Content of Session:

—Reflect on the reading:

"You yourselves are our letter, written in our hearts, that everyone can read and understand; and it is plain that you are a letter from Christ . . . written not with ink but with the Spirit of the living God; not on stone tablets but on the tablets of human hearts."

—Share with great reverence how you see Christ in each person's behavior, what virtues are evident in each person.

Note: If this is done in a group, one person receives feedback from all the others before going on to the next person.

LEVEL IV: DIALOGUE

GOAL: To experience genuine communication
TASK: To risk discussing difficult issues
FEAR: Destruction of self or group
VIRTUE: Courage

Reflection: Go to the gospel to study how Christ met persons and led them into heart-to-heart communication. These meetings seem to go through several phases, that is, relationship, communication and mutual self-disclosure.

Scriptural texts for reflection and modeling

1.	John 4:6-30	Woman at the Well of Jacob
2.	John 21:4-18	Peter's encounter with Christ on the shore of Galilee after the Resurrection; his three-fold declaration of love for Christ
3.	John 9:1-7, 35-38	The man born blind is healed of his blindness and makes his profession of faith in Jesus.
4.	Luke 24:15-32	Jesus walks with the disciples on the way to Emmaus and leads them gradually to relationship, communication and mutual self-disclosure.

Note: Follow the model or paradigm below in this reflection.

Questions:

—How does Jesus set up the climate for the relationship to develop?

—How does he communicate so that persons recognize his compassion and personal response to them? through touch? words? actions?

—What risks are involved in his response to others?

Jesus: The Paradigm for Dialogue

1. **Climate**

   His actions and words first create a climate where growth and inner healing can take place.

2. **Compassionate Perception**

   He sees people with problems rather than problem people.

3. **Personal Response**

   He responds to people where they are—physically, emotionally, spiritually, whatever their need.

4. **Relationship**

   He risks entering into relationships with others, shares himself with them and invites them to live and to grow.

5. **Dialogue**

   He confronts them with their weaknesses but calls them to life and growth.

Summary

We have been looking at experiences that can assist in building up trust levels, namely, through acceptance of self, revelations of self to others, faith sharing or sharing personal experiences of God at work in one's life, and finally dialogue.

These stages are not separate stages but rather continuous and overlapping. Developing a climate of trust is not a once-and-for-all situation. With the stresses and strains placed on people, it is imperative that everyone engage in ongoing exercises that will keep alive and vibrant the climate of trust in which dialogue may flourish.

Dialogue is the fruit of the previous levels of growth. It entails movement toward mutual understanding of one another, through sharing of feelings, ideals, beliefs and values. It engenders the ability and confidence to reach out to others in loving relationship. It calls us to be vulnerable, to share self with others and to encounter differences with respect.

Dialogue is the capstone of the building of trust at all other levels. It rests on the honesty and humility of the persons involved, the courage to risk confrontation, to express emotions, to give criticism, to set limits and to take a stand for values when necessary.

Notes

[1] *Devotions Upon Emergent Occasions*, XVII.

[2] Walter J. Burghardt, *Seasons That Laugh or Weep* (New York: Paulist Press, 1983).

[3] John Godfrey Saxe, "The Parable of the Blind Men and the Elephant."

Epilogue

We have come full circle. We conclude at the same point where we started: with Christ's prayer that you may have life and have it to the full. Perhaps the image of a circle is an appropriate one for the topics explored in the preceding pages. There is no end point or final word to be written or spoken on anger, forgiveness, self-esteem or dialogue. These are all integral elements in life's journey and one's willingness to understand and explore them can make the difference in their life-giving potential. In embracing them we are led to fuller life; in ignoring them we find life stagnates. Hopefully, through the insights you may have gleaned from reading and discussing this book you will experience greater fullness of life and joy.

Life and growth are processes that continually change and evolve, and in so doing call each person to new challenges and new experiences. It is in response to these invitations that growth continues. We pray that you will deepen the important life-giving relationships in your own life; that you have a willingness and courage to deal with your anger in a way that is not death-dealing but life-giving; that you forgive yourself and anyone whom you need to forgive, so that your life and your relationships will be full; and finally that you will choose to make growth in self-esteem a priority.

We pray that you may have life and have it to the fullest.

Bibliography

Relationships

Bellah, Robert, et al. *Habits of the Heart* (New York: Harper and Row, 1986).

Buscaglia, Leo F. *Personhood* (New York: Fawcett Columbine, 1978).

Hammett, Rosine, C.S.C., and Sofield, Loughlan, S.T. "Some Reflections on Confidentiality," *Sisters Today*, Vol. 51, No. 3, November, 1979, pp. 150-152.

Hammett, Rosine, and Sofield, Loughlan. *Inside Christian Community* (Jesuit Educational Center for Human Development, 1981).

Hassel, David, S.J. *Dark Intimacy* (New York: Paulist Press, 1986).

Juliano, Carroll, and Sofield, Loughlan. "Ministry Demands Intimacy," *Human Development*, Vol. 9, No. 1, Spring, 1988, pp. 31-34.

_____. "A Model for Evaluating Communication," *Review for Religious*, Vol. 44, No. 5, Sept./Oct. 1985, pp. 694-703.

Overstreet, Bonaro. *How to Think About Ourselves* (New York: Norton, 1976).

Polcino, Anna (ed.). *Intimacy* (Whitinsville, MA: Affirmation Books, 1978).

Sofield, Loughlan, and Hammett, Rosine. "Experiencing Termination in Community," *Human Development*, Vol. 2, No. 2, Summer 1981, pp. 24-31.

Westley, Dick. *A Theology of Presence* (Mystic, CT: Twenty-Third Publications, 1988).

Anger

Amadeo, Linda, R.N., M.S., and Gill, James J., S.J., M.D. "Managing Anger, Hostility and Aggression," *Human Development*, Vol. 1, No. 3, Fall 1980, pp. 38-46.

Gaylin, Willard, M.D. *The Rage Within: Anger in Modern Life* (New York: Simon and Schuster, 1984).

Gill, James J. "Anger, Hostility and Aggression: How to Deal With

Them in Ourselves and Others," *Human Development*, Vol. 1, No. 2, Summer 1980, pp. 36-42.

Sofield, Loughlan, and Juliano, Carroll. *Collaborative Ministry: Skills and Guidelines* (Notre Dame, IN: Ave Maria Press, 1987).

Forgiveness

Donnelly, Doris. *Putting Forgiveness Into Practice* (Allen, TX: Argus Communications, 1982).

_____. *Learning to Forgive* (Nashville: Abingdon Press, 1982).

Fitzgibbons, Richard P. "The Cognitive and Emotive Uses of Forgiveness in the Treatment of Anger," *Psychotherapy*, Vol. 23, No. 4, Winter 1986.

Self-Esteem

Burkert, William and Sofield, Loughlan. "Unwrapping Your Gifts," *Human Development*, Vol. 7, No. 2, Summer 1986, pp. 43-46.

Frey, Diane and Carloch, C. Jesse. *Enhancing Self-Esteem* (Indiana: Accelerated Development, Inc., 1984).

Gill, James J. "Despondence: Why We See It in Priests," *Medical Insight*, December 1969.

_____. "Indispensable Self-Esteem," *Human Development*, Vol. 1, No. 3, Fall 1980, pp. 26-36.

Sullivan, James E. *Journey to Freedom: The Path to Self-Esteem* (New York: Paulist Press, 1987).